The Stones
You Can't
Put Down

Joe Stewart

WESTBOW
PRESS®
A DIVISION OF THOMAS NELSON
& ZONDERVAN

WestBow Press books may be ordered through booksellers or by contacting:

WestBow Press
A Division of Thomas Nelson & Zondervan
1663 Liberty Drive
Bloomington, IN 47403
www.westbowpress.com
1 (866) 928-1240

ISBN: 978-1-5127-4855-0 (sc)
ISBN: 978-1-5127-4857-4 (hc)
ISBN: 978-1-5127-4856-7 (e)

Library of Congress Control Number: 2016910865

Printed in the United States.

WestBow Press rev. date: 07/11/2016

Contents

Preface ix

1. GPS Is Way Off 1

2. I Think I'm Golden 13

3. The Rock Star Way 25

4. The End of the Line 37

5. Alone but Not Alone Anymore 48

6. Unseen Dangers 60

7. I'm Available 71

8. Sold Out 85

9. The Grand Story 96

Conclusion 107

Acknowledgments 111

Notes 113

"Joe's story is incredible! Reading about his life made me praise Jesus for His faithfulness and grace toward Joe and everyone. I recommend this for those who are looking for a story that refreshes your view of God's grace and empowers you to talk to others about Jesus."

—Zach Griep, Campus Outreach, Area Director

"*The Stones You Can't Put Down* vividly displays the transformational power of God's grace in undeserving humanity bent toward sin. I was captivated by its real-life honesty and the unfolding nature of God's goodness to pursue man."

—Kim Dean May, author of *Authentic Christianity,*
7 Schemes of Satan, and *The Foolishness of God …*
Is Wiser Than Man's Wisdom

To my bride:
I am blessed beyond measure
that God gave me you
to run this race with.
(Nehemiah 6:3)

Preface

I want to outline a few things before we begin this journey together in the pages that follow. First things first. I would like to thank you for picking up this book and reading it. I really hope that the time you spend in this book blesses you in many different ways. It has taken a lot of time, effort, and sacrifice from so many people in order for this book to make it into your hands.

Secondly, this book was written to truly show the ugliness of sin and the glory of God and His love and mercy. I'm not entirely sure I would let anyone under the age of sixteen read it. There is nothing in this book that is offensive, but I do tell many stories from my life and am entirely real about them. There is nothing explicit and no bad language, ever, but I wanted to get the fullness of my sin out there. I think that too many times as Christians, or just people in general, we hold back and are not transparent about who we know we truly are—broken people. If I were to leave out the true brokenness of these stories, I honestly feel it would rob Jesus of the glory due Him in His amazing work in my life and yours. That is the premise of this book: the difference between one life and another, between being dead and being alive. For these reasons, I would read it through fully yourself before handing it to a young teen. But I trust your judgment. It is absolutely up to you to decide who you share this with.

Thirdly, this whole book is not about me. I do tell many stories about my life in this book, and that is the running thread that keeps our journey together down a chronological timeline, but I want this story to be about you too. I don't want you to just read this book straight through and see things only through my eyes. I want you to find the parallels between my stories and yours. I also want you to really think about and digest the Scriptures I have shared. They are there for a reason. They all tie in and show that God always has a plan and that we humans haven't been changing as much as we think we have over the millennia.

I want you to spend time thinking about and answering the questions at the end of each chapter, which are intended to give you points of reference to keep tying your "stones" into the story. They are what really help this book make sense in what it means for your life. They can end up being the difference between enjoying your time in this book and not. Don't just fly by them either. Be intentional with them and incredibly honest and transparent, whether you are reading this book alone or with a group. You have to be truly willing to face the truth if you want to see the fullness of your own story.

Take the time. It'll be worth it.

Lastly, I want you to see why this book was really written: to point hearts to Jesus. Whether you are a believer or not, please just give this book a chance. I was an unbeliever for much of my life, and I think you will see the realness of life in this book. And in that realness, my prayer is that by the end of this book you will ultimately see the love, grace, and glory of God. The Lord of the Universe is able to do amazing things with amazingly broken stories. Please keep that in mind as you move through this book. It is not a long or hard read, and I hope you enjoy it.

Thank you again from the bottom of my heart. Remember, we are on a journey *together.* This can turn out to be a game-changer for how you see your life—where it was and where it is going.

Okay! Let's do this!

Without further ado, *The Stones You Can't Put Down.*

1

GPS Is Way Off

Was there a time in your life when you thought it was the end of the line for you? You just didn't know where else to go or who else to turn to? I think most of us have been in a place like that at one point or another. You might even be thinking that you've been in that position multiple times. I know I have.

Being lost isn't a good feeling. We can all think of a time when we were lost while driving. The little lady on your GPS told you to take a right turn when there was no road, and all of a sudden, you had to take a few different turns of your own to try to correct the mistake. You found yourself driving down a back alley, wondering why your destination wasn't coming up on the right. Panic or frustration started to set in, and all of a sudden, you were yelling at a voice on your phone GPS because she didn't know where she was going and has led you into a dark place where you don't want to be!

That is what happened to me at a vulnerable time in my life. I was fifteen years old and had just gone through a rough season of life. My parents had just gotten divorced, and we had moved just a year earlier from where I had lived all my life. Even at that young age, I was giving up on myself because of turns my life took that I didn't expect it to take. I never would have admitted that anything was wrong because, well, because I was *strong* and could handle everything on my own!

Right.

I began listening to gangster rap music and idolizing the lifestyle that came with it. Drugs, sex, and money were the things I was chasing, and I started getting mixed up with things no parent would ever want for their child. I began having sex at fifteen and at the same time began smoking marijuana and drinking. My grades dropped, and—let's face it—I didn't care. I just kept a barely passing grade in school, and I was good with that. My popularity was growing. That's all that really matters in life at that age—right?

So I thought.

I was lost.

Looking back on it now, I can wholeheartedly tell you that I was truly lost—I just didn't know it then. I had let a voice tell me where to take a turn when there was no turn to take. I was cruising down a dark alley and wouldn't "find the destination" for another ten years. I'll tell you about those ten years over the next four chapters, but for now, there's a story from the Bible I'd like to share.

Raising Cain

The story is found in Genesis 4. It is a familiar story you've probably heard before if you've been around church for any amount of time. It's the story of Cain and Abel.

In the story, we see Cain and Abel making offerings to God. We're not totally sure why they were doing this, but we have some pretty good ideas. Nevertheless, they were doing it. It is a short story, so let's read it together:

> In the course of time Cain brought to the LORD an offering of the fruit of the ground, and Abel also brought of the firstborn of his flock and of their fat portions. And the LORD had regard for Abel and his offering, but for Cain and his offering he had no regard. So Cain was very angry, and his face fell. The LORD said to Cain, "Why are you angry, and why has your face fallen? If you do well, will you not be accepted? And if you do not do well, sin is crouching at the door. Its desire is for you, but you must rule over it." Cain spoke to Abel his brother. And when they were in the field, Cain rose up against his brother Abel and killed him. (Genesis 4:3–8 ESV)

Now, we aren't sure as to why God did not accept Cain's offering. There are a few different thoughts on this by theologians ranging from "Cain's offering was the wrong type," to "It was of poor quality," to "His heart was not in the right place." One little glimpse we do get about this is in the book of Hebrews: "By faith Abel offered to God a more acceptable sacrifice than Cain, through which he was commended as righteous, God commending him by accepting his gifts. And through his faith, though he died, he still speaks" (Hebrews 11:4 ESV).

God could have instructed Cain and Abel to offer up a sacrifice. Abel did so in faith, according to what God had said, and Cain's offering, while acceptable in his own eyes, was not what the Lord had instructed.

At any rate, Cain's *heart* was not in a good place. God, being rich in mercy, came to him and even asked, "If you do well, will you not be accepted? And if you do not do well, sin is crouching at the door. Its desire is for you, but you must rule over it" (Genesis 4:7 ESV). It's hard to say why or how Cain's heart got into such a bad place, but it was. God had presented a way out. I'm not sure what that would have been, but I'd bet that Cain knew.

Given that Abel's offering was pleasing to God, it would probably involve Cain checking his pride at the door, inviting humility into his heart, and talking to Abel about what was going on in his heart and what, or how, to sacrifice in order to please God in the way that Abel had. You almost get the feeling that Cain felt like he'd gotten a raw deal. With a heart that was broken by the inherent sin in the world brought about by his parents, Cain put a foot forward, but it was the wrong one. Sin was crouching at his door, ready to watch him fall. And fall he did.

With anger and bitterness from feeling like he had been dealt a bad hand, watching someone else be accepted and loved, Cain gave into the desire that was tearing down his heart, but he felt like it was the thing that was going to set him free.

Oh, how Cain and I are alike.

Lost

I was in a place feeling like I'd been dealt a bad hand in life. A broken family and the acceptance of girls and drugs came calling, as sin was crouching at my door, waiting for me to fall. I wasn't actively following God and didn't really know who Jesus was. I put a foot forward, and it was, like Cain's, in the wrong direction. I was eager to go down the path, though, leading me out of life and into darkness.

Have you ever felt this grip on your life? Or maybe you don't even know right now as you are reading these pages that your life is in turmoil and that sin is not only crouching at your door, it is watching you fall like a rock as well. And so are people around you, who can see your life falling apart even while you can't. They might even be telling you they're concerned or warning you of the bad that can come from the life you are living. But you don't listen. Neither did I.

There are just those times when you think you are on a roll. Like everything is going your way and you are living the good life. I know I felt that way for a long time. In high school, I had gotten to a point where I was selling marijuana out of the trunk of my car when I carried out bags of groceries for people while working at the grocery store in my town. I had popularity and people always wanting to talk to me—coming up to me and saying hi in the hallways of school—and I didn't even know who they were. I had girls who thought I was good-looking and were giving me the attention that I thought every guy would want. Yeah, I thought I was living the life.

It was the beginning of what I thought was a good run, but it would come crashing down. Over and over would it come crashing down, until I had blood in my eyes and nose and heart palpitations, and I wasn't sure I'd even make it through the night.

That's not where my story ended, though. It's also not where your story has to end either, if you've ever found yourself in these kinds of circumstances. Maybe you're in them right now. Or maybe you don't have a clue what I'm talking about because you've always been good or have always followed God. Or so you thought.

Stones

I have three amazing boys: Gunner, who is twelve, Ridge, who is two, and Canton, who isn't quite one yet. My middle son, Ridge, is an explorer at heart. At times he'll stand at the gate at the top of our stairs and just keep saying over and over, "I want outside, walk. I want outside, walk!" He just wants to go outside and walk and explore. One of the things he likes to explore, even though I tell him not to, is our neighbor's really nice landscaping. He will run over there and pick up these nice smooth river rock stones and carry them around the rest of the time we are outside. I'm not quite sure where he got the idea that carrying rocks around is fun, but to him, it's the best. When it's time to go back inside, he will get so upset when he has to put those rocks down. He's getting much better as he gets older, but he used to just flat-out lose it.

In a sense, I have two stones that I can't put down either. I think maybe we all do. One of these stones represents our past—all of the things that bring us to a point in life where we're forced into a decision about how our future will look. We've almost all been there. If you haven't, I suspect that at some point you will. It's your past, though. It is written in stone, and you can't do anything to change it. The past is the past. It is a stone that you can't put down. All of the things you wish you hadn't done are there—all of the things that, given the chance, you would take back, but you can't. They are a part of your story and who you are. They are not something you can leave behind. You can't put them down because they help tell your story.

Some people never get past this first stone. They never look at their life and realize that something is missing, that something is just not right and needs to change. They live their whole life holding onto this one stone and never picking up the other one—the one that is full of life and a new way to live it. They always think that *they* are their best shot at freedom and living a fulfilling life. They think they can write their own story until the end.

The "other stone" is where you went when you got to that point where you had to decide what your future was going to be about. Can you think of when that time was? Or maybe it's right now. I remember when mine was. Exactly. I'll tell you about it later. What that stone is to me now is not just the stone that I *can't* put down; it is the stone that I *won't* put down. That stone is my life with the Lord.

My life and how I know it now is living in freedom because of the blood of Jesus Christ that He freely poured out to pay for my sins and yours. It is the stone that I no longer write the story to, but He does. My story is now a part of His story, and I don't have to be the author of it because He is. This is the stone that I pray everyone gets to hold onto with all their strength. When you are no longer the author, your old stone never gets another word etched into it, and you have a new life being written on a new stone by a new Author.

These are my stones, and I want to tell you about some of the things that make them mine—about some of the circumstances and times that brought me to a place before the Lord where I knew I needed a Savior. There was no lower I could go and no way to feel besides wrecked. I think some of my stories will resonate with you. Ideally, they will cause you to draw correlations to your own life. If you haven't thought about the stone that you hold onto that you are the author of, you might start to contemplate it.

I also want to tell you about the stone of my present and my future—the stone that Jesus is writing into His story through my life. It is locked in and secure, held in my hand so tightly that nothing in this world could ever pry it from my grip—not even death. Death couldn't hold down the King that I follow, and He has promised it won't hold *me* down either, so I'm *never* letting go.

Your Stones

I believe in the power of testimony. I especially believe in its power when it is threaded with the Word of God and presented to bring Him glory. That is something that no one can ever take away from you—what God has done in *your* life. I want to hear your stories too. We all have very interesting and unique lives, and our stories need to be told. I know that my story is just one of millions of stories that, individually, mean very little. But, together, collectively, as a body—the body of Christ—they can change the world.

Stories have always been an integral part of humanity. They are how we pass along information or tell things about our family from generation to generation. Stories are even how the good news of Jesus was initially shared in the first century before the Scriptures were written. Stories are powerful and can alter emotions and be truly amazing.

Along with this book, there is a website, www.TheStonesYouCantPutDown.com, and a place for you to tell your story. Its sole purpose is to build up other believers, encourage people who might be in the same place as you were, or are, and to be a lighthouse for the world to see what the power of the Maker of the universe can do when you open the door and invite Him in.

Don't be ashamed of the stone you can't put down. There is reason for your suffering, and God can turn to good the bad decisions that you've made. I know what it's like to feel like no "churchgoer" can speak to me because they don't understand what it's like to still be high on ecstasy and drunk when strolling into church on Sunday morning to see if what I'm looking for is there. But guess what? There *are* people like that, and God can use my mistakes for His purposes because there is a young man sitting in a pew or chair right now thinking that same thing. And there's a way that God will use you to glorify Himself and to draw others to Him through you and your story, your stone. So don't hide that stone. It draws more attention to the stone that you won't put down.

In the book of 2 Corinthians, Paul writes,

> For this light momentary affliction is preparing for us an eternal weight of glory beyond all comparison, as we look not to the things that are seen but to the things that are unseen. For the things that are seen are transient, but the things that are unseen are eternal. (2 Corinthians 4:17–18 ESV)

Paul was seemingly always in the midst of trials. He had to always carry around the stone of his past that he had authored. But the stone of his present and future that Jesus was writing was worth so much more. So much more that, even with all the things he had been through in his life, and even with all of the things he was going through in his new life as an apostle of the Lord Jesus, he speaks of those trials as the lightest of burdens compared with the eternal glory that awaited him.

Paul's stone of the past wasn't the end of his story; it wasn't mine either, and it doesn't have to be yours. God can use you in the story that He is still writing. Just know that you can quit being the author of your story right now. The stone of your past that you wrote can end today—without another word put on it. You can pick up the stone that Jesus will write for you and experience a life worth living right now.

Off Track

The GPS named (enter your name) might have you off track right now; you might be missing your destination and not know where you are. The same thing happened to me. I was way off course. I mean, *way* off course. I was eighteen years old and had just gotten off the phone with my dad, who I hadn't talked to in more than a year. All he wanted to tell me was that he was out to breakfast that morning and the table next to him was full of police. He had overheard their conversation. They were talking about *me*. They were watching my house for drug trafficking.

What are some times in your life where you really felt like your GPS was way off?

What correlations can you draw between Cain's story and yours?

If you've never experienced trusting Jesus, what does the stone that you are authoring look like?

If you have placed your trust in Jesus, how do your two stones differ?

2

I Think I'm Golden

You've been on a roll before. You remember what it was like. No matter what you did, you got away with it. You not only got away with it, you had fun doing it, and nothing was going to stop you from doing it again. You might even push the envelope a little further the next time. You might be right in the middle of one of those rolls right now. But those rolls don't ever last.

There is a wall out there somewhere, and everyone—and I mean *everyone*—ends up hitting it. But before you do, you think you are the golden child. Everything is about you, and for you, and at your disposal in life. It's all for your entertainment and your personal gain. And you love it. Listening to God is an afterthought. It might not even be a thought at all. And if He did come calling, you sure wouldn't listen. On this roll in your life, when you are the golden child, this life is about you and what you want, not what God wants. You are fleeing from God and not looking back.

Jonah

At the beginning of Jonah's story, he did the same thing. His story starts with exactly that: hearing from God and not listening.

> Now the word of the LORD came to Jonah the son of Amittai, saying, "Arise, go to Nineveh, that great city, and call out against it, for their evil has come up before me." But Jonah rose to flee to Tarshish from the presence of the LORD. He went down to Joppa and found a ship going to Tarshish. So he paid the fare and went down into it, to go with them to Tarshish, away from the presence of the LORD. (Jonah 1:1–3 ESV)

We aren't completely sure why Jonah didn't listen to God and why he fled from Him. There are a couple of good and strongly speculative reasons why he didn't, but when it comes down to it, does it really matter? He didn't listen!

Like I mentioned before, you might have experienced a time when there was no way you could even hear from God because you were so wrapped up in yourself. How could you possibly hear God's calling into your life?

We almost all know the next scene in the story of Jonah. A great storm came and scared the daylights out of the other guys in the boat, and after a short string of events, Jonah was thrown over the boat and into the belly of a huge fish. After three days, Jonah got out of the fish and ended up going to Nineveh, but seemingly not willingly.

Sound familiar?

Have you ever found yourself in a tough spot when your run was hitting the wall and you were, for once, not so into yourself that you heard God calling you and maybe thought, *Okay. I'll go. But only because you just got me out of the belly of that fish.* Reluctant obedience.

Jonah's story doesn't end there, though. He got to Nineveh and told them what God had asked him to say, and then he left and set himself up on a hilltop to watch the destruction of the city he didn't like. But Nineveh took to God's warning and turned from their ways. So "God relented of the disaster that he had said he would do to them, and he did not do it" (Jonah 3:10 ESV).

At the very end of the story, we see Jonah being incredibly ungrateful—so much so that he's asking God to just kill him. After all that God had brought him through, still all Jonah thought about was himself and what he wanted, not what God wanted. The belly of the fish wasn't enough to warn him not to turn from God. So he ran.

So do we.

Pastor Tim Fritson talks about ungratefulness in this story by saying, "We become ungrateful when we think our momentary blessings are eternal guarantees."[1]

Too many times we get our warning or our momentary blessing and think it is an eternal guarantee. Jonah got his momentary blessing when he got out of the belly of the fish, and you received your momentary blessing or warning, whichever it may be, and thought it was all you needed to escape what you were in. Did you listen? Did you listen for the long haul? Sure, Jonah listened. But only to get to the next chapter and become ungrateful.

I'll bet that at some point in your life you have done the same thing. You got a warning, in one way or another, and either heeded it—just to turn your back and become ungrateful later on—or just basically ignored it altogether.

My warning came in that phone call from my dad. But before I tell you about what happened that night or after it, let me lay out for you how I got there.

The Fall

Once I had started partying and getting the acceptance I was searching for, I was hooked. But being hooked on partying and acceptance didn't end there. I was smoking pot daily and drinking four to five nights a week. By the time I was sixteen, I was doing cocaine occasionally on the weekends, and by the age of seventeen, I was all in. Pot, alcohol, cocaine, ecstasy, mushrooms—you name it. If you had it to do, I was going to do it with you. It made us friends, right?

Well, taking part in all of those things isn't a cheap lifestyle. I didn't like the idea of stealing, and working minimum-wage jobs wasn't going to pay my car insurance or cell phone bill and allow me to keep partying and have cool things.

After thinking about how I could get more money in my pocket, I decided I should stop paying for the drugs. Not because I was going to quit doing them but because I was going to sell them. So I got started. I bought my first quarter-pound of marijuana to sell. It went fast.

In the little town where I lived at the time, getting rid of marijuana wasn't a hard job. I turned that quarter-pound into a half-pound, and a half-pound into a pound. I had money rolling in—so much that I didn't know what to do with it. I mean, I thought I knew what to do with it. I bought all the new AI sneakers (if you're under the age of thirty, you probably don't even know what AI's are, huh?), lots of new cologne, a DVD player, movies, clothes, and anything else I wanted. But that wasn't enough, though.

I wanted to make more money. I was originally from Iowa and had a lot of friends who still lived there and went to a university there. So I decided to start taking pounds of marijuana to Iowa because marijuana prices were way higher there than they were in Kansas City.

I did that for a while, but the road was lonely and the risk seemed too big, so I decided that if I started selling other things instead of just marijuana, that would cover the money I would lose from not traveling up to Iowa anymore. I made new connections and started selling cocaine—and mushrooms too. For a brief period of time, I would leave the Kansas City northland and my nice suburban town and go down to the inner city of KC to get crack cocaine to bring back and sell for the few who wanted to try it.

My life was torpedoing out of control, but, like I mentioned earlier, I was the golden child. Nothing could happen to me.

My story to this point might be way different from yours. But can you think of how you might have been flying right past every red flag and every yield sign, heading straight for destruction, but didn't realize it or care? Maybe it wasn't drugs and money for you. Maybe it was status or popularity. Maybe it was the acceptance of the opposite sex in ways reserved for marriage only. Maybe it was pride or judgment, thinking that you were better than everyone else and that they needed to know it. Maybe it was work, or pornography, or apathy. Whatever it was, there were plenty of times when you probably thought, *I should get a grip on this and quit.* But you didn't. Neither did I.

The Call

My "belly of the fish" moment came one evening when I received that phone call from my dad. I had run away from my dad's house when I was sixteen and went to live with my mom. I loved my mom and still do, immensely, but the main reason I moved over there was because I had no rules. You parents know that sometimes a dad is just able to demand more respect and obedience than moms. When Dad started to realize what was going on in my life, he started laying down rules, and that was enough for me. I was out of there.

One morning I got up, packed my stuff, and left for my mom's. The evening prior to that was the last time I would speak to my dad until the night he called me more than a year later.

The call was obviously unexpected. Most of our warning signs are, but don't they have to be in order to get our attention? "Jonah had gone down into the inner part of the ship and had lain down and was fast asleep" (Jonah 1:5b ESV). He wasn't expecting that his life was getting ready to change. He was fast asleep! He was running from the Lord and totally unaware of what lay in the moments ahead.

I had just got back from making a run to sell something when my mom came into my room. She handed me the phone and said, "It's your dad." I said, "Hello," and he informed me that he had visited this local diner for breakfast that morning and the table next to him was full of police officers from our town. They were talking about some things, and when he heard my name, he really started listening.

Long story short: they were watching my mom's house for drug trafficking. To this day, I don't understand why cops would be talking loud enough at a local diner about such serious issues. It would have been tough for my dad to have made that up, not really knowing what things I was into because of our lack of communication for the last year. So I believed him.

I took all the drugs I had, called all the people I knew, and had a "going out of business" sale. I got rid of everything I had that night and thought, *No way they're getting me. No way they're bringing down the Golden Boy.*

Warnings

That warning came—and went. Many of us do the same thing. If you're like me, you need to be brought to a place of total despair, and I wasn't there yet and wouldn't be for some time. A lot of us do that, though. We get knocked down but not knocked out of our senses, so we just keep going. We do what we think will get us out of the predicament we have gotten ourselves into and breathe a sigh of relief. About five seconds later, we are ungrateful, and instead of searching for the "light of the world" (John 8:12) in Christ Jesus, we stroll right back into walking in darkness.

Do you remember what it was like in that place? Are you going through it right now? It's just constant uneasiness and doubt. Stress rules most days, and a lot of days you just want to give up and give in. But then there is the day or two where you'll hit that stride again and tell yourself, "That was fun!" and you can't wait to do it again. Don't let anyone tell you Satan doesn't give you anything because he absolutely will. He isn't stupid, and he's been making fools out of us since the garden of Eden. Even Christ called him the "prince of this world" (John 12:31 NIV). Satan offered Jesus the kingdoms of the world, saying, "All these I will give you, if you will fall down and worship me" (Matthew 4:9 ESV).

Jesus knew better and leaned on the Word of God instead of listening to those sly false promises. Satan will give you things—but only to hook you and then tear the rug out from under you. How foolish we are when we think we will not fall for the tricks of a jester who has been tap dancing on the fallen souls of men for millennia. He was laughing all the way to the bank when I blew right through the warning sign with little regard.

Ignoring the Warning

I had plenty of money left over from my time dealing drugs to last me quite awhile without having to change my way of living it up, so it was just a minor setback. I was happy just to had gotten rid of all of the drugs I had, thinking I had outsmarted the law.

I worked a couple of jobs, went to a type of vocational school to get my certificate in personal training, and worked at a gym in Kansas City for a couple of years. The party never stopped, and it just started to pile up. I was making decent money as a nineteen- to twenty-year-old and had my own apartment. I was young and fit, had some money and my own place, and a new addiction—girls.

The drugs and alcohol didn't go anywhere at all. They remained a staple in my life, especially weed. That was an everyday thing for me. Not just *every* day, but *all* day, every day. Like five to eight times a day. As long as I got my workout in, the rest of the day was spent finding time to get high.

But next to that addiction was the one to girls. Texting girls all day and going out to meet new girls every other night. It was an empty cup that was never filled. Going from bed to bed is no life to live, and unfortunately, I was one of those people.

The story of my life kept playing the same tune for most of my time as a personal trainer until I was twenty-one. I had enrolled and dropped out of college, kept partying, and kept entertaining my fleshly desires. Then, at the age of twenty-one, things started to change—and not in a good way, either.

But I had not yet hit the bottom of that canyon to think I needed anything outside of myself.

I got a new job one month after turning twenty-one that paid really good money—*really, really* good money for a twenty-one-year-old with a bunch of bad habits. I was on a 1:00 p.m. to 9:30 p.m. shift. I could sleep in every morning and go out every night. Now I had money to take my party life to a new level and started taking weekend trips from time to time to different cities just to party in different places. I had no desire to slow down, get into a committed relationship, or think about the future. The present was all I cared about.

Obviously, though, as much fun as I thought I was having, something was missing. Something was always missing. A life like that is an endless pursuit for happiness that never brings the fullness of life and joy that a human being knows deep down that he or she is made for.

I started dating a girl off and on just to have some kind of consistency in my routine and feel like someone needed me.

Around April or May 2007, I visited my family in Colorado. Though no one had a clue exactly how out of control my life had become, it probably wasn't hard to see that I needed help. Others can always see when you are in need of help more than you can. They would call me weekly and tell me they were praying for me and telling me the Gospel over, and over, and over, and over, but I wasn't listening. But don't think for a second that it didn't speak truth into my heart over and over again that would resonate with me later in life.

I pray that someone is speaking that into your life right now. Do you know who that person is? If so, you should listen.

If you aren't in that place right now because you are walking with Jesus, trusting in Him, and doing the best you can to follow God's will, you should think of the person, or people, who did that for you. Then you should think about who you should be doing that for right now and then do it. They need you. They can't see where they are heading, and you know the God who can save them.

I love my family. I wanted a mini-break from the party for a weekend, so I went to visit them and relax. I was in the Denver airport, about to board my flight home, when I got a phone call from the girl I was sort-of dating. She said the two words you never want to hear as an unmarried—and not *planning* on getting married—guy. The two words that could totally bring this golden child down to earth.

I said, "Hey." She responded, "I'm pregnant."

In what ways have you, like Jonah, displayed a reluctant obedience toward God?

Recall a "belly of the fish" moment in your life. Did you listen to it or fly by it?

Who were, or are, the ones voicing warnings to you about where your life was/is going? Thank them.

Who should you be warning and speaking truth to right now, someone living only for their self-authored stone?

3

The Rock Star Way

It was a long flight home. I didn't know what to think, as thoughts raced through my head faster than a NASA rocket heading into space. What should I do? Should I marry her? Should I bail out and move somewhere? I didn't believe in abortion (still don't), so I was just lost on what to do.

When I got home, we got together and talked about our situation. We knew we were going to go through with having the baby and were going to try to be together to provide a "normal" atmosphere for the baby.

After a short time of contemplating what to do, we decided it was time to tell our parents. They were all actually supportive. I had made up with my dad since The Call. He was disappointed, but the more the prospect of a grandchild got to him, the more excited he got too. My mom was consistently supportive through it all.

Thinking at this point that it was time to grow up and be a man because I had made decisions in life that were reserved for a man, I thought that the most responsible thing to do in this situation was to get married and make it work. After talking about it and weighing our options and what was best, we decided that was the route we would take.

So, at twenty-two years old, with an unexpected pregnancy and a relationship hardly built on love and trust, we got married in my dad's backyard. Only a handful of family members were there—no friends, no real wedding ceremony with the flowers, pictures, and guests. Nevertheless, it was real, and it was an oath before God—not that I thought of it in that way at all, though.

After finding out about the pregnancy and up to the wedding day, I knew I was in a tough spot, so I started trying to read the Bible a little bit and ask God for His help. I read Bible studies, a couple of books, and prayed a little bit. My dad had always taken me to church when I was a kid, so with nowhere else to run, I decided to run that way. It was short-lived.

Looking back, it was only for my own personal gain. Don't a lot of us do that? Here I was again, with my back against a wall for the second time in my young life. I had wised up a little bit, I guess, and knew that, obviously, when I tried to work things out for myself, absolutely nothing had gotten better. I looked to God for help, but I looked for help to get me out of the mess I was in—not to *know* Him.

Think of a time when you might have done the same thing. You were between a rock and a hard place and didn't know where to turn and were just flat-out exhausted. You knew that if you relied on yourself again, things wouldn't get better, and you thought, *Maybe God will get me out of this.* Was it out of a desire to know Him, or just a desire for your life to be easy and go back to the way it was when you were enjoying whatever it is that you were doing? Mine was for the latter reason.

A few weeks had passed since we had gotten married. We were living in an apartment-style basement in her mom's house, and I was thinking, *This might just work out.* We had our first appointment to get a sonogram to see our baby for the first time. I took the day off work, and we got in the car, drove to the appointment, and waited in the waiting room. Finally, our name was called to go into the back. She got settled on the table, and they got the little wand out and started rubbing it around on her stomach. And there it was: nothing.

It turned out that the baby had died at about the peanut stage. The pregnancy sac had grown like it was supposed to, but the baby had not. We were devastated. A couple of days later, we were in the hospital for her to have the procedure to remove the remnants of the pregnancy.

Nothing after that went well for us. She treated me as ugly as you could treat someone, and rightfully so. We cussed and yelled at each other. I went straight back to smoking pot all day every day and going out after work and getting drunk and coming home at 1:00 a.m.

Everything was a mess, and we were both lost. Eleven months after we were married, we were divorced. Just like that—another failure in life.

You might be reading this book and thinking that you can relate to many things I have been through. Some of these stories might seem eerily familiar to how your life is going right now. Yours might not be the exact same story, but you can draw parallels from it and see the same chain of events happening in your life.

If that's the case, where are you turning for your comfort and purpose? Are you leaning on drugs, or maybe sex? Are you seeking out the acceptance of others, or even calling on God to make it all better and take it away? Maybe you've said this before: "God, if you just fix this for me, I will never do anything like this again"—only to eventually get out of that situation and then go right back to what you were doing without a second thought. Or maybe you had a second thought but the pull of whatever it is you wanted was stronger than your pull to live for and love a holy God.

Adulterous Israel

Our stories are very similar to that of ancient Israel's. God had chosen them as His people to show the world what life was like to be living for the one true God. He led them out of Egypt in the most miraculous of ways and was going to bring them to a land that He had promised their ancestors. But not long after the very beginning of their journey, they'd forgotten about how God had rescued them. They wanted more, and they wanted it now. They were yelling at their leader, Moses, saying,

> "Would that we had died in the land of Egypt!
> Or would that we had died in this wilderness!
> Why is the LORD bringing us into this land, to
> fall by the sword? Our wives and our little ones

28

will become prey. Would it not be better for
us to go back to Egypt?" And they said to one
another, "Let us choose a leader and go back to
Egypt." (Numbers 14:2–4 ESV)

Israel would repeat this sequence of events more than
once. They would call on the name of the Lord, only for Him to
answer them faithfully because of the covenant He had made
with their ancestors. But the people would just continue to
worship idols, turn from Him, and run from Him.

When I was reading through the Old Testament earlier
this year, I sat and thought to myself how foolish these people
were. It was obvious to me that God was trying to help them—
but they just kept running from Him.

Now I can see that I am no different from Israel. I'm
guessing that you can see that you are no different from Israel
either. What will it take for you to follow God with all your
heart and all your life and leave these false idols and this life
of stress and shame behind? What will it take for you to be
the hands and feet of Christ Jesus to someone you know who
is going through times like these right now and needs your
help—someone who needs to know the Gospel? Are you just
too busy or too comfortable to take the time out of your life
to be that person for them?

Back in Action

I moved out of my ex's mom's house and got an apartment
in the northland of Kansas City. I reconnected with a few

friends who had really started to get into the club scene in downtown KC, and I was back in. I still had not hit that wall in knowing that I needed God. Swifter than a Usain Bolt two hundred meter dash, I was back in the mix and back to the only way I knew how to live (or so I thought). But this time it was a little different. I was in my early twenties, and I had a job that made good money and a host of friends who were happy to welcome me back.

The next three years of my life were a whirlwind—a constant sprint to the next night out, the next girl, the next drug, the next club, the next satisfaction. I was on a chase to live like a rock star. And in my eyes—and in those of the group I ran with—that's exactly what we were.

Through a series of connections and meeting new people, I had a group of friends who could go anywhere and do anything in the Kansas City club scene. Countless nights of VIP bottle service at clubs and indulging in too much ecstasy and cocaine to count. I was among a bunch of guys in their early to mid-twenties who knew every club manager or owner in the city and had unlimited privileges. We were all more successful monetarily than anyone should be at that age and had no moral compass. And that made for a lot of trouble.

It didn't take long for the "Do you know who I am?" mindset to kick in. I thought I was better than everyone, and there was no way *your* crew could even come close to hanging with *mine*.

We were rock stars.

In *our* minds, at least.

No one I ran with would blink an eye at dropping $500 on one night out, and we all did it pretty regularly. I'd get my check on Friday and pay my bills—some of them, anyway—and the rest was for partying. By Sunday morning, I would always be out of money, and the funds for any partying I was going to do on Sunday or during the week had to come from the ATM at QuikTrip. I always went to those ATMs because they would let me overdraw my account. Partying was the priority. VIP everywhere, New Year's Eve at Playboy parties in Chicago, over-the-top weekends at Lake of the Ozarks, nonstop. I remember a couple of times I thought I should just stop and think about where my life was going.

But I didn't.

A few of my old friends from up north had come down to visit me for a weekend, so I thought I'd show them how we rolled. I showed them a night of partying and an after-party at my friend's house until 6:00 a.m., and my friends from Iowa didn't know what to think. They were like "That was fun, but I don't have any desire to do that again. You do this every weekend? You *live* like this?"

Things kept rolling along just like that. In a single night at the club, I remember taking four and a half ecstasy pills, one cap of GHB, a large amount of cocaine, and an uncontrolled amount of alcohol. Looking back, I have no idea how my body handled those things. No idea.

One Saturday in the summer of 2010, we were partying during the day at a rooftop pool in Kansas City. The same old story was playing out: girls, alcohol, and drugs. I had left the pool around 4:00 p.m. with a friend and a couple of girls. We went back to his house to continue partying and get cleaned up to go back out that night.

I have no idea why I did most of the stuff I ever did. We thought it'd be fun to take GHB and shoot 9mm pistols in the backyard of my friend's house. In a *neighborhood*. No more than twenty minutes later, there were six cop cars at the house. Except for weed, the drugs were gone. One of the girls put the marijuana in her purse, and my friend hid the gun. Well, the police found the marijuana, a pipe, and the gun, and everyone got arrested—except *me*. It was my friend's gun, so he got arrested for that. Each girl had weed or paraphernalia hidden in her purse, so they got arrested for that. And I wasn't under arrest for *anything*.

After all the cops had left, I hung around the house for about an hour. I then decided it was time to go bail my friends out. I didn't get one block from the house, and there was one of the police cars. It's like they knew I was going to leave, and they weren't going to let me get away with anything. They took me through the roadside sobriety steps. Somehow, I passed them all.

Even after that, I was under arrest for suspicion of DUI. I was promised that if I blew under the legal limit of .08 on their extra-high-tech machine when we got to the station, I would be let go.

When we got to the station, I sat in a cell with my friends for a bit, and then they called me out to blow. I don't know how long it had been since my last drink, given all the things that had happened between leaving my friend's house and sitting in front of this machine at the station. But whatever the case was, I blew.

In an almost amazed, vividly annoyed manner, the officer's face changed. He turned the screen around to show me: 0.79—a *hundredth of a point* from being canned. I was soon on the phone with a buddy, and he was on the way to bail out the rest of my friends and pick us all up. (My car had been towed after being pulled over)

I had slipped by again. It was my fourth arrest, but I'd never spent more than a night in a cell, so I guess it didn't faze me. I'd like to say that my life changed the next day when I got out of there, but it did not. Not in the slightest.

Your Story

I am burdened to know that my story is not the only one like this. So many today live in the same state of dismay and pain. Sure, the nights of partying and pleasure seem fun—just like I mentioned before, the devil will give you some things you desire to keep you away from the Savior, who wants you to have true life. But after those nights, the mornings are empty and alone. That pit in your heart will not be quenched by anything other than the love that comes from God.

He formed you in your mother's womb. He knows the number of hairs on your head. He has numbered your days, and each one of them has a purpose. And if you will just listen to Him and give Him your all and follow Him, He will lead you into a life you couldn't imagine—not a life of glitz, glamour, and luxury, but a life of purpose and worth that invests you in a kingdom that is not of this world.

I pray that if you have made it this far in this book and are not yet following Jesus Christ with your whole life, you would consider it. I pray you would seek to know Christ—to seek the face of the Lord, to know Jesus, and to not turn from Him but listen to Him and trust Him. Hebrews 3:15–4:1 says it better than I can:

> As it is said, 'Today, if you hear his voice, do not harden your hearts as in the rebellion." For who were those who heard and yet rebelled? Was it not all those who left Egypt led by Moses? And with whom was he provoked for forty years? Was it not with those who sinned, whose bodies fell in the wilderness? And to whom did he swear that they would not enter his rest, but to those who were disobedient? So we see that they were unable to enter because of unbelief. Therefore, while the promise of entering his rest still stands, let us fear lest any of you should seem to have failed to reach it. (ESV)

My hope and prayer is for you to quit rebelling and being disobedient and to pray against unbelief. I pray that you believe. If you do, I pray that you follow Him with an unrelenting heart—not with a *portion* of yourself but with *all* of yourself. And I pray that it doesn't take you what it took for me to seek Him.

The Beginning of the End

It was Halloween weekend 2010, a weekend like any other—I was partying and trying to live like a rock star the best that I could. For whatever reason, though, through all of the nights and drugs I had done in my life that my body had no problem handling, this time was different. By Sunday night, I was left on a couch in my house with blood in my eyes and coming out of my nose, vomiting, eyes twitching, and an irregularly beating heart that I couldn't get under control. Something was different this time. Something was wrong. I didn't know what to do, who to call, or where to run.

For the first time ever, I actually acknowledged my mortality.

I was scared.

When have you seen similarities between adulterous, forgetful Israel and your life?

Reflect on Hebrews 3:15–4:1. What jumps out at you about this passage?

Are you struggling with unbelief? If your answer is yes, explain.

If your answer is no, are you following God with an unrelenting heart? Explain.

In Chapter 3, you answered the last question with a person who was living for their stone. Have you prayed for him or her or reached out to him or her yet?

4

The End of the Line

The weekend started out the same as it usually did—with me partying. With as many times as I've had to write that so far, I feel like this is a broken record. How could one's life so easily dwindle down to one thing? Unfortunately, life ends up that way for so many.

It was Halloween weekend. I went out to the clubs that Saturday night with a large group of people and the girl I was "somewhat dating" at the time. I remember getting into an argument with her and our night out *together* ended early, but not the night out. I continued to party with friends until about 2:00 or 3:00 a.m., and then we had an after-party at our house.

I slept for two or three hours. Then my roommate and I had got up at about 7:00 a.m. to start getting ready for the NFL Chiefs game later that morning. We started drinking beer and had run out of cocaine, so we started taking Adderall pills we had lying around. We left the house to head down to the stadium to tailgate and—you guessed it—party.

On the drive down, we collectively drank a fifth of Grey Goose vodka. We arrived at the stadium and started drinking beer to tailgate. We stayed for the game and had a couple of girls back over to our house after the game. At some point or another, the girls had to leave, and we decided that we were going to stay in for the night for once. We got some marijuana out and kicked back to watch some Sunday Night Football.

Something wasn't right, though.

I didn't feel that great, and for some reason, it just kept getting worse and worse. It got to a point where I couldn't take it anymore, and I ran to the bathroom and threw up. Usually that would make me feel better when I release that awful feeling. But this time, it didn't help anything.

Once I was finally finished, I got up and got cleaned up, rinsed my mouth out, washed my face and hands, and looked in the mirror. I saw blood coming out of my nose, and my eyes were beyond bloodshot. I could hardly see them. They were just completely red—no white in them at all.

I finished washing up, headed back into the living room, and lay down on the couch. Things didn't start to get any better, though. My heart was racing, and I couldn't concentrate on trying to get that under control because my eyes were twitching, darting around the room, pretty much out of my control. I was trying to focus on my heart, though. It had started beating really irregularly and feeling like it was going to explode.

There I was, lying on the couch, blood in my eyes and coming out of my nose, eyes twitching, heartbeat irregular, and thinking, *This is it.* My roommate offered to take me to the hospital, but I declined. I always thought it best to take the consequences of my own decisions. If the decisions that led to this point in life were the end of the road for me, so be it. In my twisted logic, I'd rather die on that couch than go to the hospital and have someone tell me I had overdosed and was a drug addict, or whatever the case may be. So I stayed there on the couch.

After more than an hour in this state, I did actually start coming back down to earth. I was downing water and lying on the couch, concentrating on getting my body under control. Around midnight, I was starting to feel confident that if I went to bed and fell sleep, I would live. I did go to bed that night, and obviously, I did live.

When I woke up in the morning, I called into work. I was up in my big, loft-like room in the upstairs of our house. I was contemplating the night before and running through different scenarios in my mind. *How lucky am I to be alive? What if I would've died? Who would've cared? What would have happened to me if I had died? Were heaven and hell real? Was Jesus real? Do I even care about the answers to any of these questions? Should I just go downstairs and roll another blunt and forget about the whole thing and keep the bus rolling like I always have in the past?*

I decided to actually think about a couple of those questions a little more intentionally before making a move. *What if God was real? If I had died, would I have gone to heaven or to hell, based on the life I have lived thus far?* I quickly concluded that if I had died, I would have gone to hell and missed out on heaven—if it were real. And if it were real, so is eternal life— one that lasts forever.

Think about that: eternity. That's a really long time—a longer time than any human being can even begin to start getting their mind around. I tried to, anyway, and it felt like a dark cloud was forming around my soul. I realized that in my own afterlife, I would spend a trillion lifetimes in an empty despair, apart from God, in a place of torment and darkness, away from the One who created me and gave me life in the first place.

I really did start to get scared and fear God. *What am I doing—living life away from Him? The Being who spoke creation into being is available to know and follow, and I'm living like this? God said, "Let there be light," and light came screaming into existence at 186,000 miles per second, and I haven't been fearing Him?*

I was scared again and knew I had nowhere to go. Nothing I could do would help me or the situation that I kept finding myself in. I was done. I had reached the end of the line.

The Prodigal

There's a very familiar story in Scripture that I absolutely love. It reminds me much of myself. I can't believe that Jesus was telling parables about foolish people in His time, and here I was, two thousand years later, still living in the same kind of despair that humans have been giving into for almost our whole existence.

Jesus tells us of someone in a similar situation. This guy thought he had life figured out. He was on top of the world, living the life he wanted to live and thought he deserved. He was The Man. But life would come crashing down, like it always does.

Many people know it as the parable of the prodigal son as told in Luke 15:11–32. We won't do a deep expositional study of the passage, but if you'd like to—and I strongly recommend it—you should read Timothy Keller's *The Prodigal God*.[2] It is phenomenal, as is all of Dr. Keller's work.

At any rate, Jesus begins the parable by telling us about a man who had two sons. The younger of his sons asked him to give him his share of the family estate, his inheritance— which is a big slap in the face to his dad, given he's not even dead yet! But the father does it anyway. He must have been a pretty loving father.

Jesus then describes the younger son's actions after getting his boatload of money.

> Not many days later, the younger son gathered all he had and took a journey into a far country, and there he squandered his property in reckless living. (Luke 15:13 ESV)

The NIV translation of this verse even says, "Squandered his wealth in *wild* living" (Luke 15:13, emphasis added). It doesn't hit home for me much harder than that right there, and it should hit home for you as well. Even if your life wasn't as reckless as mine up to this point, any life outside of the will of God is reckless or wild living.

What do we plan to accomplish by ourselves? What kind of kingdom are we attempting to build for ourselves? And what kind of logic can we possibly muster for living within our own rules and ways and not by the ones laid out for us with love and wisdom by our Creator? Stress and heartache can almost be guaranteed sooner or later—but usually sooner—for those living under their own parameters.

That's what this guy had chosen for his life, just like many of us—reckless and wild living. But his luck had run out, and he had hit that proverbial wall. He had spent everything he had. It doesn't say how long it took him to spend it all, and I kind of like that. By not mentioning the amount of time it took for the young man in the parable to reach his depths, the parable frees you to think about your own time frame. It took me ten years to end up in this place. Maybe it took you ten months. Maybe it took you twenty years. Or maybe you just moved out of your parents' house, had your first taste at living on your own, and decided you were going to live by your own rules and your own reasoning, and it took you only ten *days* to get to this place of need.

The passage tells us he spent everything. Everything. For real—*everything*. Maybe it doesn't say it like that, but I'm saying it like that. It goes on to tell us, "He longed to fill his stomach with the pods that the pigs were eating, but no one gave him anything" (Luke 15:16 NIV).

He got to the point where he had hired himself out for work, and his job was to feed pigs. He ended up being so hungry that he wanted to eat the food he was feeding to the pigs. You don't think this guy tried everything before getting to this point? I bet he did.

I bet he spent all of his money. I bet he had overdrawn the ATM to the point that a laughing clown face showed up on the screen when he put in his card. I bet he borrowed everything he possibly could from the so-called friends he had made during the time he was in the money and buying every round. And I bet he burned every bridge possible to any meaningful relationship he had to keep himself sitting high on the pedestal of life and to look good. Yeah, I bet he did everything he possibly could to keep up with the Joneses before selling himself out and wanting to eat out of a pig trough.

Ever been there? Maybe not with drugs or money, but with status and pride? Ever burned relationships, told lies, exaggerated the truth just so you could stay in your self-proclaimed spotlight just a little while longer?

Well, this guy had. And finally, he'd had enough. Jesus tells us that this young man had decided that he had hit the end of the line, and that it was time to give in. Jesus tells it this way:

> But when he came to himself, he said, "How many of my father's hired servants have more than enough bread, but I perish here with hunger! I will arise and go to my father, and I will say to him, 'Father, I have sinned against heaven and before you. I am no longer worthy to be called your son. Treat me as one of your hired servants.'" And he arose and came to his father. (Luke 15:17–20 ESV)

He finally saw his need for more than he could get for himself—and not in the sense of money, or prosperity, or friends. He needed some food, and he needed life. He needed his father. So did I. And so do you. Our eternal Father is who we need.

The young man did head back home, probably with his head hanging lower than we can imagine. He had an "I'm sorry" speech planned out and was going to offer himself as a worker to his dad just so he could get paid as one and get some food.

In a beautiful display of grace, as he was kicking rocks down the dirt path on the way to his dad's estate, "his father saw him and felt compassion, and ran and embraced him and kissed him" (Luke 15:20 ESV). Before he could even finish his thought-out apology speech, his father cut him off and hollered to his servants,

> Bring quickly the best robe, and put it on him, and put a ring on his hand, and shoes on his feet. And bring the fattened calf and kill it, and let us eat and celebrate. (Luke 15:22–23 ESV)

He had made the long—probably *really* long—walk home with thoughts of fear, shame, and embarrassment clouding his head. He wasn't even to the gate. He was still way off in the distance, maybe just barely recognizable on the horizon. His dad saw him, and contrary to what the son had thought, his father had been waiting for his son to return since the day he'd left. He ran out to him, something a man of respect would not do in that time, squeezed his son, loved him with everything he had, and rejoiced in his return.

In a conversation later in the parable with the elder son (whom we did not talk about here), the father goes on to say about his youngest son, "Your brother was dead, and is alive; he was lost, and is found" (Luke 15:32 ESV).

The Comeback

If you haven't figured it out yet, the son in this story is me (and you), and the father in the story is God. And like the father in the story, God is waiting for you, with arms open wide and forgiveness an ocean deep. He loves you with a love that is unmatched and unbroken, and He wants you to come home.

No matter what you've done. No matter how low you think your life has fallen or how unlovable you think you are, all you have to do is start home. Jesus has paid the price to have you and to give you life. He has what it takes to give you freedom. He won't just meet you where you are. He will run to you. He will hold you in His loving embrace and celebrate the return of His child.

You are loved. You were bought with a heavy price and are cherished by the King. Louie Giglio, in his book *The Comeback*,[3] puts it this way when talking about this same parable:

> These stories are crossing the lips of Jesus, God in human flesh come to pay the price for our freedom. No one is getting off scot-free. Jesus is taking the blows for our wrongs, satisfying the wrath of a perfect God, and paving the way for us to be completely new in his love. Sure, the younger son always lived with the fallout of his decisions. But right beside him

the whole way was a Father whose compassion and forgiveness gave him strength to walk in confidence and humility into a brand-new future.

There I was, in my room. It was November 2, 2010. I had racked up a decade of bad decisions, countless drugs, so many reckless choices, too many girls, countless fights, four arrests, one dead friend, who knows how much money blown, a life with nowhere to go, and flat-out lost.

I had contemplated the questions in my head. I had prayed, for the first time in who knows how long, and I just gave up. I gave in. I had reached the end of the line. I knew that I was wrong and that I wanted true life and believed that the only way to get it was with Jesus. I just asked him, "Jesus, I am wrong. I believe. I can't do this. Help me. I need You. I need a Savior."

I needed a Savior, and there He was. Right before me the whole time. Waiting for me to turn to Him. And there He was, running to my side, to scoop me up and call me His.

Before I even understood what grace was, I had found it. I was dead but was brought to life. I was lost and now was found.

What comes to mind when you think about eternity?

Have you ever exhausted every possible option, clawing to keep the limelight on your self-authored stone? If so, what did that look like?

Do you remember the moment when you decided you were done being the author of your life, your stone? Explain.

If you haven't, do you think it's time?

5

Alone but Not Alone Anymore

Up in my room that day, my life changed forever. It was like Jesus spoke into my heart and let me know that I was His. I had been baptized back when I was twenty-one, during that brief time when I was seeking Him, but I was quickly drawn back to the desire of sin and worldly perspective. I won't get into how critically important I believe it is to follow the direct command of Jesus and be baptized, and how it has been modeled throughout church history, but now I felt like I was fully surrendering, not only obeying. I had a new outlook, a new Author, a new life. I was holding a new stone.

The next few months of my life were 180 degrees from the previous ten years. Besides marijuana, which I kept smoking intermittently for the next few weeks, I never touched a drug again. I quit going to the clubs, and the Lord even placed it on my heart to clean up my language and stop cursing within the same few weeks that I quit smoking pot.

I would sit up in my room and read Bible stories and soak in what the Word was speaking to me. It was love being spoken right into my heart. I would sit and watch YouTube and Vimeo, listening to sermons from Louie Giglio and Francis Chan. (If you aren't up on these two gentlemen, you need to be). All I listened to was Christian music in my car to keep my heart clean and reminded of Christ's love while I was driving. David Crowder and MercyMe became my favorite music, a stark contrast from the gangster rap and techno I was accustomed to.

I could go on and on about how much God changed my life in that short time over the winter of 2010–2011, but I'll spare you the ooey-gooey details—although I think that wouldn't necessarily be a bad thing. Too often I think we forget what it's like to be in love with God, in love with our Savior, who paid the price for us to live true life. We forget to chase after Him like we would an earthly relationship. It's a choice we have to make. Choose to love the Redeemer of your soul, and follow after Him with all you have!

I was on cloud nine almost all day and night. But I was alone. I was alone in the sense that my phone went silent, my Facebook page was blank, and the Bible and Netflix were my best pals.

Something that might be holding you back from giving your life to Jesus is just that—loneliness. Just like the young man in our story of the prodigal son from the last chapter, once the bottles stop poppin', the money quits spendin', and the smoke (literally) clears, you find yourself standing alone. Sort of back to where you started. Back to where you were when you first started searching out the things that had gotten you into the circumstances you were in. But this time it's different. This time you're not all alone. This time, even though you may be standing in an empty house, the presence of the Universe Breather and Life Giver is there with you. And you have rest, real rest—the kind of rest that leaves your soul in peace and your life in a place of agreement with how it was intended to be.

Saving Saul

I was thinking about this as I was writing the other day and thought, *Who else in Scripture might have experienced the same thing?* Now, I could be way off in left field on this one, so e-mail me if I'm totally wrong, but I think I've got something here.

Saul.

Saul was the biggest hater of Christians on the block back in that day. He'd wreak havoc to keep the Gospel from spreading. Matter of fact, he'd hold your coat for you if you wanted to stone a believer of Christ to death. To death!

But things changed for Saul one day when he wasn't expecting it either. He was on the road to Damascus, "so that if he found any belonging to the Way, men or women, he might bring them bound to Jerusalem" (Acts 9:2 ESV). If you were a believer, he was on his way to find you. It was different from what my life was, but Saul was an enemy against God nevertheless.

Things changed for him when he encountered Jesus on that road, though.

> Now as he went on his way, he approached
> Damascus, and suddenly a light from heaven

shone around him. And falling to the ground he heard a voice saying to him, "Saul, Saul, why are you persecuting me?" And he said, "Who are you, Lord?" And he said, "I am Jesus, whom you are persecuting. But rise and enter the city, and you will be told what you are to do." The men who were traveling with him stood speechless, hearing the voice but seeing no one. (Acts 9:3–7 ESV)

Umm... awkward. After that, these guys traveling with Saul had to literally lead him by the hand in order to get him to Damascus because when Saul opened his eyes, he couldn't see anything. He'd been blinded. The Christian killer had been brought to his knees, for all they knew, by a voice in the wind. Now his traveling companions had to lead this guy, whom they probably well respected and were glad to accompany, like a child. And they were speechless.

Oh, I'm sure they had plenty of thoughts running through their heads. I'm sure Saul had plenty of thoughts running through his head as well. Maybe there was a little awkward conversation about what had happened after they'd gotten a little way down the road. But I'm betting those guys couldn't wait to get Saul to Damascus and get away from him.

Now, at the same time, a disciple named Ananias in Damascus had a vision in which the Lord told him to go to a house where he would find Saul. Ananias understandably did not want to do that. He responded to the Lord, "I have heard from many about this man, how much evil he has done to your saints ..." (Acts 9:13 ESV).

The Lord made a quick reasoning to Ananias. Like you should always do if the God of the universe speaks to you, Ananias did what He said. So Ananias got up, went to Saul, and laid hands on him. Saul was healed and was filled with the Holy Spirit. They rose up, and Saul was baptized.

Think about those first three days for Saul—maybe even longer. Who knows what the dynamic was between Saul and Ananias those first few days of their God-ordained relationship. I'm sure Ananias was still a little weary around him. Saul probably felt a little awkward having to be helped and loved on by this guy he had just met and who was one of the people whom just the week before he was persecuting. But Jesus was in the picture. And when Jesus is in the picture, you are never alone.

I'm sure their bond strengthened quickly because they had Christ in common now. I'm sure they talked about Him all the time together. I bet Ananias introduced Saul to his friends, and "For some days he was with the disciples at Damascus" (Acts 9:19 ESV).

Saul had gone from being a loner, left in a city by his escorts, to being cared for and loved by the people of God. Now Saul had a brotherhood around him. He went to speak at the synagogues, proclaiming Jesus, saying, "He is the Son of God." Those people couldn't believe what they were hearing because they knew Saul had been the "havoc bringer" to the name of Jesus and now was a microphone for Him.

New Loner to Heart Donor

You can be led to assume that in the time that passed between verses that Ananias and/or the disciples in Damascus were discipling Saul. He may have gotten direct revelation from Jesus, but these guys were still taking him in and ministering to him. Despite his flaws, past, sin, and reputation, they were loving him and pouring into him. Ananias listened to the Lord and made the first move. And the church was there to help.

I know this is not necessarily an exegetical way to look at this section of Scripture, but just think about the realness of this story. By the spurring on of the Lord, Ananias went out on a limb for someone into whom he would've never put time—maybe even someone that he would've run away from. But Saul was broken. He had nowhere to turn except to where Christ had called him to go, and he found himself alone, until the body of Christ picked him up and set the love of Jesus on him. And the transformation that took place in Saul, who would later become Paul, was extraordinary. We see him pour his heart and his life into the Kingdom of God.

This can happen all around us. I'm not saying we shouldn't be discerning, but when the Spirit is calling you to love someone, bring the love of Jesus to him or her—even if you don't know them. He or she may not be in your Christian bubble, or maybe you know some dirt on them that drives you away. But fueled by the forgiveness and love of Christ, stories change every day. His or her story might be changing right before your eyes, and God might be calling you to be a part of that. Jesus could be calling you to help transform a new loner into a heart donor.

Is this something that happened to you? It could be something that God is calling you to right now, and you might be saying no. I know I have failed at this too many times to count. I see someone I don't know at church who looks like he or she might be there for the first time, and I don't leave my bubble to be an Ananias. The truth of the matter is that we are called to make disciples. That doesn't just *happen*—you have to be *intentional*. If we are called to make disciples of all nations, don't you think the *easiest* place to start doing that is in your own church at least?

Praise God, He ordains these opportunities to love others. We are all broken, just in different ways. Discipling someone, or being discipled, is a beautiful thing. Play your part in what God has called you to and the people you know you should be loving. Don't leave them feeling alone in a house built for God.

In a sense, I think we can relate to Saul. I know I can. In those first few days and weeks after meeting Jesus, I felt kind of alone. No one was calling or asking me to hang out anymore when I quit being about the things of this world. I was full of joy and couldn't believe how it felt to know Him, but He has built us to live that out with *others,* and I didn't know any "others."

Hi, My Name Is ...

I visited a church in Liberty, Missouri, not far from where I lived and where I currently reside called Desperation

Church. I started going there and felt the weirdness (that's a good thing!) of how much love was there. The worship was amazing, the preaching was sound and captivating, and the people are those who serve.

I met a guy named Jamey Overby who really took me under his wing to show me Christlike fellowship. He introduced me to the pastor, Michael Kraft, and these guys got me connected into meeting other guys at that church, serving the community in various outreach activities, and being part of the men's group there.

Christ has built His church to be a body. If you aren't in a local gathering of believers, you are missing out on how Jesus has intended your life to look. We will talk about community later on in the book, but just know that Jesus knows better than you. If He has set up His Bride to be a *body* of believers—not just a bunch of people out there trying to do it all on their own—He probably has some pretty good eternal wisdom for doing it that way.

It was great to be connected to these guys, this church, and to start to distance myself from my past. I made a new friend who was my age, David Fulton, and started spending time at the young adults study he was leading. I was learning more about who God is and what that meant for my life.

There is one thing I do want to say about that time in my life and what I think it can mean for you too. I absolutely had to distance myself from my past in order to get away from it and not be tempted in the ways that had held such a tight grip on my life for so long. I think that you need to do that too. Whatever it is that has kept you from loving God and following Jesus the way the Word calls you to, I think you need to get away from it. You need to grow with Christ and have a union with Him that is bonded in eternal things before going back to those areas to speak life into others.

I know now that I am not my own. I am bought with a price higher than I could ever pay and given a life and purpose larger than I could ever imagine. And because of where I'm at now, I am more than comfortable being in any place and talking to anyone, in the sense that now my heart is burdened for those who are into the things I was chained by. But I know it was key for me to distance myself from that while I was growing in Christ. Before I would be able to be used for His purposes in circumstances where those old chains could be clinking, I had to get away from them for a while.

It had been several months since that day in November, and I was growing more and more in love with the Lord. I started praying about God giving me someone to run this race for Him with—someone to hang out with, share things with, and go out on dates with. But now I didn't know how to meet one. Without the clubs, alcohol, and drugs, I didn't know how, or where, to meet a girl I was attracted to and who was into the same things as me.

Being the impatient man I still am today, I decided to do something I never thought in a million years I would do. *Only old people and people who are desperate would do that,* I thought. But I decided to give it a try. I went to an online dating website called ChristianMingle and built a profile because they had an ad that let you do that free for one week. I didn't know that, at almost that same moment, there was a pretty little lady about twenty-five miles from me doing the exact same thing.

I wasn't hip to the idea of meeting someone online, so I almost never went online during that week I had the free trial. But on the very last night that it was available, at about 9:00 or 10:00 p.m., before they shut the free messaging down and I would have to pay for it, I got on. I scrolled through the names and pictures, not excited about anyone I was seeing in particular. But then I saw this lady, Rachelle. I thought she was really pretty and thought I'd give this thing one chance and one chance only, so I messaged her and said, "Hello." I waited for about five or ten minutes and received no reply. I thought, *Great. This thing doesn't even work or is already turned off.*

I gave it one more try, though, and this time, she messaged back. She said that she hadn't responded the first time because she was five years my senior and thought maybe I was too young for her. But we talked that night for about three hours.

For whatever reason, the site let us stay on past midnight and we eventually exchanged phone numbers. We called each other the next night and talked for about another three hours and decided that, the following week, we would have our first meeting at a restaurant in Liberty. The date went well, and we started being exclusive shortly thereafter.

We started dating and attending church together, meeting each other's families, and becoming not just boyfriend and girlfriend but also best friends. I'll fast-forward through the rest of our dating life to three months after we started dating to when we took a trip to Colorado for her to meet my dad's side of the family.

I had it all planned out. We went to Bear Lake, up in the Rocky Mountains, one of the most beautiful places in the world, if you ask me. I had enlisted the aid of people she didn't know to stay hidden with cameras and video recorders. And we walked. We walked away from my family and around the lake to a little clearing where there was a bench that overlooked the mountain and the lake. I told her that we should sit down and just look at the beauty in the mountains. She went around and sat on the log bench, but I did not join her. It actually took her more than a moment to realize that I had not sat down next to her, but she finally did and turned around to see what I was doing.

I hadn't left. I was there. I was just behind her, on one knee, with a ring in a box and just one question for her.

Did you experience a loss of any kind when you turned to the Lord? Explain.

Have you ever been disobedient to the leading of the Spirit in pouring into someone?

Are you discipling someone or being discipled? If not, what are you waiting for? (It's not just a one-time gig.)

How did it feel to begin to let the Author of life write your story on your new stone?

6

Unseen Dangers

Rachelle and I had dated for only three months when I asked her to marry me. I know that might not seem like a very long time to some, but for us, it was right. We knew we weren't getting any younger, we were attracted to each other, and we had the most important thing in life in common: Jesus. I knew that I wanted to spend my life with her and that she was the woman for me. So after three months of dating and a three-month engagement, we were married on September 30, 2011. We did not see the point in prolonging that part of our lives together, and I'm glad we didn't. As I'm writing this, we have been married for more than four years now.

My bride is the most precious gift God has given me in this life. She stands behind me in support of all we do. She is a prayer warrior, an obedient daughter of the Lord, and an inspiration to me and many others. Our (and your) marriage is the first display to the world of the good news of Jesus Christ. Love your spouse with more than you can muster—and then love them some more!

That first year of marriage, though, was not the honeymoon phase that some people make it out to be. We had a lot of learning to do. She was a single mother when we met, so I was learning how to be a parent and to lead a family. She was learning how to have someone lead her because for the last seven years, she'd been the head of her house. It was rough. One thing that made this first year tough was our search for a church home.

We had purchased a house in Liberty, Missouri. We were both rooted in our own churches where we came from, so with both of us being a tad stubborn, neither of us wanted to give up our church home to go to the other's church. Petty as it may seem, it was nevertheless an issue for us.

We got some Christian counsel on the matter and were told to look into finding "our" church—not hers or mine, but somewhere that was *ours*. This turned out to be a taller task than we expected, an unseen danger we had not even thought about in our new life together: trying to learn about how to walk with Jesus as a married couple.

For eight months, we went from church to church, visiting and leaving. Some were okay, but it felt like there was no love in the room. Some simply did not preach the truth of Scripture, and that is not what we were looking for. I don't want to dog any other churches, but it opened my eyes to what is considered Christian in America.

Too many times, we think of "being Christian" as just being more moral than the next guy. "I have morals, and I go to church, so I'm a bona fide Christian." This is far from what Jesus meant by saying, "If anyone would come after me, let him deny himself and take up his cross and follow me" (Matthew 16:24 ESV). In our Americanized Christianity, I think that too often we forget that the first-century church did just that. Almost all of the apostles lost their lives defending and spreading the name of Jesus. They weren't worried about if their society frowned on it. This is the eternal Kingdom of God we are talking about here. We're not selling Girl Scout cookies, and we should not be afraid to ask if someone wants to buy some. It makes sense why Jesus followed up that statement with "For whoever would save his life will lose it, but whoever loses his life for my sake will find it" (Matthew 16:25 ESV).

Community

We did, however, find a church, Liberty Christian Fellowship. Just like plenty of other amazing local churches around the world, it's a place where the love there was weird—and that's exactly what I think it should be. It should run so counter to culture that an outsider would just have to wonder what in the world is wrong with these people because of their love for one another. This should be a love that we share with every other follower of Christ on the face of this planet. It should be *obvious*—especially real and tangible in the local church you are a part of. It's why Jesus says,

> A new commandment I give to you, that you love one another: just as I have loved you, you also are to love one another. By this all people

will know that you are my disciples, if you have
love for one another. (John 13:34–35 ESV)

Did you catch that? "As I have loved you" is what Jesus said.
He came down from His rightful position in heaven and lived
on this earth and died for you! If you want to be critical of the
text, you could say, "Well, He hadn't died yet when He said that
to the disciples." In a chronological time frame, sure—but He
had been literally sharing His life with His disciples. They
did everything together. They traveled, ate, talked, prayed—
everything. Are you doing that with your local church body?
Are you joining in fellowship and community with the other
believers who make up the body of Christ in your area? The
book of Acts tells us how believers in the first century were
toward one another.

And all who believed were together and had all
things in common. And they were selling their
possessions and belongings and distributing
the proceeds to all, as any had need. And day by
day, attending the temple together and breaking
bread in their homes, they received their food
with glad and generous hearts, praising God
and having favor with all the people. And the
Lord added to their number day by day those
who were being saved. (Acts 2:44–47 ESV)

They undoubtedly loved one another and were willing
to share their lives with one another, and it made a huge

difference in how God chose to use them to add to their number daily. Are you in a community like this? If you're not, shouldn't you be? Shouldn't church be more than a Sunday and maybe a Wednesday night? Is it biblically okay to just flat-out say, "I'm just really busy," or "I'm too tired"? Is it not important enough in your life to delegate time for? Community is huge. Jesus said so, and it's how He set up His church to be. Think about that.

Rachelle and I really appreciate this church. It was led by a wonderful man who quite frankly rivals anyone I know as a genuine person with love in his heart, Pastor Kim May. He introduced himself to us within the first two or three times of our visiting there. This was no small task either, as LCF (Liberty Christian Fellowship) is a church of more than fourteen hundred people.

We started to get plugged into LCF and into a small group and other things, when around that time another danger I didn't see coming crept in.

BCB

Rachelle's brother had a country-rock band called The Bryant Carter Band. The guy who used to book their shows for them had moved, and they asked if I could help out with it. I'm very lucky in the sense that I really love all of my in-laws. I am blessed to be in their family, and they have been wonderful to me from the beginning. I dearly love them all. I thought it would be fun and a good way to make some good memories with my brother-in-law, Bryant. So I agreed.

This happened around May 2012. I had no idea what I was doing, but I like challenges and trying to figure things out, so I got started on my new hobby. One month later, they played the first show that I booked for them at a place in Grain Valley, Missouri, called Whiskey Tango. It was the band's first time playing there, and they had a crowd of almost two hundred, which was a really good show at that time. (They already had a pretty decent following).

I don't know how it happened or how I figured it out, but in no time at all, we were playing two to three shows a weekend, and by October of that year, I had landed them a gig opening for ZZ Top in front of more than three thousand people.

That jump-started somewhat of an obsession for me in trying to get the band signed and playing the biggest shows possible. I really believed in the quality of the music, as Bryant is the most talented songwriter I've ever heard, and the members of the band (Shawn Buxton, Jake Franklin, and Ben Wemhoener) are exceptional musicians.

The next two years can be summed up as "The Bryant Carter Band" years in my life. I worked nonstop on this goal of managing the band to success. I provided the shows and the logistics. They went out and displayed amazing musicianship and played great music. We accomplished more than we ever thought we would in a short amount of time.

From that show in October 2012 with ZZ Top, we went on to play shows and be on tours we never thought possible. We opened for John Michael Montgomery, Mark Chesnutt, Diamond Rio, Billy Joe Shaver, and others. We got to play multiple dates on Aaron Lewis's "The Road Tour" and multiple dates on Grammy

Award-winner Reckless Kelly's "Long Night Moon Tour." We played more than a half-dozen shows with Rounder Records recording artists Blackberry Smoke, more than a half-dozen shows with the Randy Rogers Band, and multiple shows with one of the fastest-growing country acts in music, The Turnpike Troubadours. We toured from South Dakota to Texas, and while some of it was hard and long days on the road, we made a lot of good memories and had some amazing experiences.

While that was going on, something had shifted in my life, though. I continued to study the Bible through those two years, and Rachelle and I went to church and small group when I was in town. And our small group and church loved us so much through that time, bringing us meals when our son Ridge was born and again when he was in the hospital for a week with RSV at just a month old. They loved us with the love that I touched on earlier in this chapter. But we had not made that a priority.

My leadership of my family, or lack thereof, had slowed our devotion to Christ, or moved it into idle at best. I had let something come between my life and Jesus and had hardly even noticed it. My work with the band had become my top priority, not my walk with my Lord. I was more interested in selling the next CD or booking the next show than I was with taking the Gospel to people.

Wanderers

How often do we do this, and so unknowingly? James 5:19 begins by saying, "If anyone among you wanders from the truth ..." I think in life we do that a lot more than we think. We wander. And though I had let myself wander and idolize something other than Christ for a long stretch of time, I think we do this almost daily.

How many opportunities do we let slip away where the Holy Spirit has just set us up for a perfect opportunity to share Jesus's name, but we have an excuse as to why we shouldn't right then? How many times do we think we just don't have the energy or the time or the resources to do what we know we are called by Jesus to do? Do we not think that God is worth it or that He will provide the words? Or do we all just struggle with unbelief more than we would like to admit to another believer? I think portions of all of those questions are true in my life, and if you search yourself, probably in yours too.

One of my best friends, Ben Wagenaar, was over at my house just last night, and we were discussing this very thing— the struggles or temptations that arise in life and how soon we forget the Father's love for us. We forget that Jesus spilled His blood so we may live in victory over sin and death and that the Spirit that rose Him from the grave lives in us and reminds us of these truths (Romans 8:11). But when we let our guard down and don't live with the armor of God (Ephesians 6) engaged in our lives, that is when we most easily fall and unbelief and doubt creep in. And when unbelief and doubt creep in, that's when sin abounds in our life.

We forget about our need for Him and start to think that our work, family, entertainment, desires, social media, food, sex, vacations, or pride outweigh the benefit that only He brings. We soon forget that He is who fashioned us in our mother's womb and that He is who knows everything about us and gives us true meaning and life.

Psalm 139 reminds us of how deeply our Father knows us.

> O LORD, you have searched me and known me! You know when I sit down and when I rise up; you discern my thoughts from afar. You search out my path and my lying down and are acquainted with all my ways. Even before a word is on my tongue, behold, O LORD, you know it altogether. You hem me in, behind and before, and lay your hand upon me. (Psalm 139:1–5 ESV)

These truths were recorded thousands of years ago and are exceedingly available for us to know, but at times, we choose not to. I had chosen not to during that season of life. I was the exact thing we talked about at the beginning of this chapter. I was a churchgoer, but not a Christ follower.

End of the Road

As quickly as the band had started up and taken off, it became evident it was coming to an end. We were all tired of the long miles on the road and the nights away from home. I was getting tired of working a full-time job and then heading out of town almost every week for shows and missing my wife and (at the time) two boys. Bryant was offered a job in Texas, not music related. It was a great career opportunity, so wisely, he took it. And just like that, The Bryant Carter Band was no more. Bryant still writes and records amazing music in his spare time, but there is no more band and no more shows.

I transitioned back into normal life and loved my free time and new time with my family. But with all those hours that I had spent the last two years sending e-mails, taking phone calls, setting up shows, etc., I now had nothing to do.

Praise God, He used that bittersweet time in my life to call me closer to Himself. I started taking the time that I was spending on booking shows and investing it into reading books or listening to sermons and taking notes. I had fallen deeper in love with my Redeemer. I was on fire for knowledge and getting to know Him better and trust my relationship with Him more, but there was so much I didn't understand about what it truly meant to follow Him.

I remember it like it was yesterday. It had been a couple of months since the band had ended, and I was just doing my daily studying, listening to a sermon, and taking notes.

I loved to learn and loved to hear the Gospel told by all these amazing pastors, but this message hit me different. It hit me in the core and made me finally see what it was that I was missing in my life—following and obeying my King.

It was a sermon by Pastor Louie Giglio. It contained two words that I think, in this society, we are very scared to let out of our mouths and proclaim to God. It was a sermon that challenged me to raise my white flag and pray, "I fully surrender. I'm available."

Are you truly loving the people of your local church?

How could you be doing better to display the love with which Christ loves you to your local church?

What unseen dangers have crept into your life at one time or another and distracted you from the Kingdom of God? Explain.

Reflect on Psalm 139:1–5. What feelings come up when you realizing that God loves you and cares for you this deeply?

7

I'm Available

It was in December 2014. I was listening to a sermon titled "Comfort Must Fall"[4] from Louie Giglio on my headphones while at work. That's what gets me through my long days at work mostly—sermons by my favorite pastors over my headphones. At the end of the sermon, he was challenging the listener to do something that might be out of the norm for a Christian in America these days: to proclaim that "God is big" and that all of these other things in life are small in comparison to Him. In proclaiming that, you are acknowledging to Jesus that you are available. You are available for His purposes and will give up your life for His cause and His glory, whatever that looks like.

This floored me. Not that it was inherently profound or something that I hadn't technically known to do, but rather something I had never really done, heard, or thought completely necessary to do.

Doesn't God already know I'm available? you might think. I initially thought that too. But He wants to hear from you. He loves you and desires a relationship with His children, just like a father desires a relationship with his kids. I might know that my stepson, Gunner, loves to play basketball, but I want to hear all about it. I want to know the moves he's learning. I want to know who his favorite player is or how his practice went. I want to hear from him, and God wants to hear from you.

David expresses in Psalm 8 the astonishment that he has in that the God of the cosmos wants to personally hear from him and cares for him.

> When I look at your heavens, the work of your fingers, the moon and the stars, which you have set in place, what is man that you are mindful of him, and the son of man that you care for him? (Psalm 8:3–4 ESV)

He loves you and wants to hear from you. Rest assured, He does hear you. First John promises us that the Father listens to us.

> And this is the confidence that we have toward him, that if we ask anything according to his will he hears us. And if we know that he hears us in whatever we ask, we know that we have the requests that we have asked of him. (1 John 5:14–15 ESV)

Is it not safe to say that He wants to hear from us? Is it not safe to say that you being available for His work and His kingdom delights His heart and abides in His will? Let us not just presume that we don't need to say out loud that we are available for Him—we need to do it. He wants you to obey and He wants you to pray. The prophet Samuel had a word for king Saul about obeying and presuming things back in the book of 1 Samuel.

> But Samuel replied: "Does the LORD delight in burnt offerings and sacrifices as much as in obeying the LORD?" To obey is better than sacrifice, and to heed is better than the fat of rams. For rebellion is like the sin of divination, and arrogance like the evil of idolatry. Because you have rejected the word of the LORD, he has rejected you as king. (1 Samuel 15:22–23 NIV)

Be obedient. Delight in what the Lord has for you. Tell Him you are available for His purposes. Say it out loud. Don't assume that it doesn't need to be said out loud. Take the time to do it. Like right now. Put the book down, and pray about this and what it means for your life. Tell your Father that you are on board for His agenda.

But What If ...?

If you didn't take the time to do that or just don't want to right now, what is the underlying reason? I don't know what yours may be, but looking back, before I exclaimed that to God, it was something that I may not have really thought about but now realize was a host of things that kept me from praying that prayer.

What would that do to my life? What if He calls me into something I don't think I'm ready for? What if He leads me to move across the country? What if He asks me to move across the world? What about the Netflix shows I want to catch up on or the leisure time I enjoy? What if He cuts into my personal time for those things or just in general, for myself? What if I'm called to give more of my money?

Are your concerns similar? Maybe you are afraid that He will lead you to spending less time on your career. Maybe He will lead you to spend more time engaging in conversation with unbelievers and proclaiming His name and fame, and that scares you. Maybe He will call you deeper into relationship with Him and His church, and that sense of opening up and becoming part of a deeply rooted community makes you queasy. Or maybe you are just too wrapped up in yourself, your family, or your friends to really seriously care about what He truly wants from you right now. Maybe if you're being honest with yourself, you think that you've got it all under control right now and that you don't have time to see what God's calling is for you.

Life Laid Down

Well, that day I prayed that prayer. I asked God to use me however He saw fit. I told him that I wanted to follow Him at whatever the cost. In order to find the fullness of life that only Jesus can offer, we must be fully willing to raise that white flag, to say, "I'm available," and find true life when we lay ours down. We truly follow Him when we give up our own life in response to His. This mirrors what Jesus said in Luke 14:27, "Whoever does not bear his own cross and come after me cannot be my disciple" (ESV).

I shared this sermon "Comfort Must Fall" and "I'm Available" prayer with my wife, Rachelle, and we started praying this together. As God would have it, we had an opportunity to really focus on this when, just a week or two later, our couples small group leaders, Jake and Katy Wylie, announced that we would start the year 2015 with a study on prayer.

To begin that study, every couple in the group needed to come up with their major prayer request for the year so that at our second meeting as a group in 2015, we could share together what our major prayer was going to be. Well, needless to say, Rachelle and I knew what our request was going to be: to be available.

Let me tell you, God has turned our lives upside down since we started fervently praying that prayer to Him. I remember talking to a friend of mine who is not a believer, telling him about how God is shifting our lives and saying, "You have to see how awesome this is. That either God is being entirely faithful to us praying this prayer, or we are living the most ironic lives ever right now."

Within just a couple of weeks of praying that prayer, God had started a work in our hearts and in our lives that would forever change our outlook on Him and on how we serve Him. It started by having seemingly increasing opportunities to speak the Gospel, and the courage to do so, which led to wonderful conversations about Jesus with guys who didn't even like the thought of church. And then just weeks later, they and their families were sitting next to us at church.

Just a couple of weeks later, our associate pastor, Tim Adams, came over to us after church one Sunday and asked us if we would pray about taking over as leaders of the young adults ministry. The couple who had been leading it for the last four years was being called into ministry in Eastern Asia as full-time missionaries, and our name kept coming up for taking over the leadership of this group.

We couldn't believe that out of the fourteen hundred people at our church, the leadership at our local church would be prayerfully led to ask us. Mind, blown. We did pray about it, and we did say yes, knowing that it was God's calling for us and His faithfulness to our being available for Him. It has been the most wonderful experience, and every person who walks through our front door and comes to open the Word of God and talk about Jesus with us has been such a blessing to us.

We transitioned into that role, and in the midst of that time, an opportunity was presented for me to go to India for two weeks on a vision trip and to engage the lost there. We prayed about this a lot. We knew it would be quite a sacrifice for us, as our new baby, Canton, would be only four months old, and we just really didn't have the money to afford it.

I have to admit that the thought of going to India did excite me, but it also brought in those thoughts that we talked about a few pages ago. What about Rachelle having three boys to look after alone while I was gone? What about all the time I would miss from work and the money we would lose? What about that time I would lose with my infant and toddler at such bond-forming ages? (I knew Gunner would understand, being twelve and my being able to talk to him on the phone at night when I'd call Rachelle).

Again, through prayer and following what we were led to know was His will for our lives, in spite of all the questions and worry, we committed to my going. We knew it would be a sacrifice on all those levels, but following God is never guaranteed not to be. We just had faith.

There honestly was no way we could afford for me to go, though, and we just knew that if we weren't willing to go deeply into debt for it to be a reality, we would have to raise the support to go. Again, God was faithful. He quieted our doubt in epic fashion when, in less than two months, we were fully funded. He lifted the burden off our shoulders and put it onto His. He showed us His faithfulness yet again. Not only did He do that, but He really showed us His faithfulness through His people. It is beautiful when God's people are willing to sacrifice for His cause.

The day came for me to leave, and my family took me to the airport. I flew from Kansas City to New York and then all the way to Delhi, India.

God moved in so many ways while I was there with our team, and it was one of the most challenging, yet wonderful experiences of my life. Rachelle and I are feeling called to those people full time in the future, if the Lord wills.

I won't get into great detail in this book about the whole trip, but I would like to share just one story with you—my favorite memory from the trip, although it's hard to narrow it down to just one. It was an unannounced interaction as we were just walking the streets and were given a precious opportunity to speak truth and the name of Jesus into a couple of lives.

Shoeshine

My great friend, Brad, and I were walking through a market area in Mumbai, honestly with not much of an agenda because the rest of our team would not arrive until the next day. Two young men approached us, Bebo and Deepak, asking to shine our shoes. We found out that this was not an uncommon request, but we had running shoes on—not exactly the type of shoes you need to be shined.

We said, "No, thanks," but they followed us, asking us what kind of store we were looking for. They assumed we were there to shop. We explained we were not there to shop but instead were there because we love people. This must've intrigued them because, for close to two hours, they followed us and talked to us. They spoke decent English, so it was easy to communicate.

After a long stretch of time, Bebo said, "Please don't be offended, but may I ask you a question?" When we said, "Of course," he asked, "Would you be so kind as to buy me a box?"

He went on to explain that he wanted this box because it came with a certificate to be a cobbler, to work on shoes on the street side and not get ticketed by the police for unlawful business. He told us his dreams were to get this box, work hard, save, and then one day open a shop of his own. He said that if he got this box, it would change his life. The only thing he needed to change the course of his life was this box and how much it would mean to him.

"You can change my life," said Bebo. But we had to explain to Bebo and Deepak that nothing we could do would truly change their lives—that they needed much more. It wasn't material, and it wasn't going to be found in a box. We said we were sorry, but we would not be buying their box for them, but for good reason.

Brad asked him what he had done so far to get this box. Bebo replied, "I prayed to Ganesh every morning for four months." We asked how that was going for him. He said, "Ganesh no listen." We went on to explain to them that Ganesh does not listen because he is not real, that he is no god at all. I asked if they knew who Yeshu (Jesus) is, to which they responded, "Oh, yes—we know Yeshu. We pray to Him too!" This is what you sometimes run into when speaking with Hindus.

"No, no. Only Yeshu," I replied. We explained to them that only Yeshu hears prayers and can answer them. Brad then began to lay out the Gospel for these guys and explain what it meant to believe in Jesus. Then we asked if we could pray with them.

So right there, in the middle of the market, with too many people to count surrounding us and some listening in closely, we prayed. Brad prayed over them. And while we were praying, I was just being pulled by the Spirit to display a great faith for Him to these guys.

Where Is Your God?

See, I had just recently done a study on faith and a great story on that was given in 1 Kings 18:20–40. It tells the story of Elijah confronting the prophets of Baal on Mount Carmel. He showed great faith in knowing that their god was no god at all; he worshipped the one true God, and, when he prayed to his God, He would listen.

Elijah bet the prophets that their god could not call down fire to the altar and burn their sacrifice and that *his* God would answer the call of His servant. For hours, the prophets of Baal cried out, and nothing happened. Not even a spark. When they finally gave up, Elijah said, "Oh yeah— now it's my turn to show you who power is!" He didn't actually say that, but I'm sure it crossed his mind. He rebuilt the altar and even had people pour water on it to make it impossible to set fire to and display the power of God. The Word tells us:

> And at the time of the offering of the oblation, Elijah the prophet came near and said, "O LORD, God of Abraham, Isaac, and Israel, let it be known this day that you are God in Israel, and that I am your servant, and that I have done all these things at your word. Answer me, O LORD, answer me, that this people may know you, O LORD, are God, and that you have turned their hearts back." Then the fire of the LORD fell and consumed the burnt offering and the

wood and the stones and the dust, and licked up the water that was in the trench. And when all the people saw it, they fell on their faces and said, "The LORD, he is God; the LORD, he is God." (1 Kings 18:36–40 ESV)

Faith

What an awesome display of faith. This was what was being pressed into my heart while Brad was praying over Bebo and Deepak. So when we finished praying, I felt God had led me to ask them how much money it took to feed their families for five days. They said it took about twenty rupees a day. I gave each of them one hundred rupees apiece and told them, "This will feed your families for the next five days. In those five days, Brad and I will pray to Jesus that you end up getting your box. Not from us, but from some other way. And that when you get it, you will know it was Jesus who answered the prayers of His servants and that He is God and worthy to be praised and Him alone."

Brad and I left them with that, and we prayed. We prayed as soon as we got around the corner, in a gas station parking lot, and we prayed for the next five days that God would reveal Himself to them and that they would get their box and recognize Jesus as their Savior.

We will probably never know on this side of eternity if they got their box. But as Elijah had faith, so do I. I believe God was faithful in making His name known and shifting the lives of two families that were once lost and now could know Him.

The Only Boast Is in Jesus

God has continued to move in Rachelle's and my life, and we are continually blown away by Him. As I'm writing this, I have an opportunity to speak at a juvenile center in two weeks, and I am beyond excited about sharing the hope of Christ with these young people, who are on the same life path that I once was. Our young adults group has grown, and God has opened doors for us to start giving God's love to South Asian Indians right here in our home city.

But I say all of this to not boast in anything at all that Rachelle and I have ever done or will ever get to do. Please, I beg you, don't forget where my life was at the beginning of this book and what my life looked like when I tried to do things my way. I am a lost cause without the grace of Jesus Christ. We boast in nothing but this truth and know that our fruits are just the outflow of His Spirit in us—nothing of our own accord. The apostle Paul says it much better than I can in the book of Galatians.

> But far be it from me to boast except in the cross of our Lord Jesus Christ, by which the world has been crucified to me, and I to the world. (Galatians 6:14 ESV)

I only want this chapter to drive you, in love, into seeing what is possible with God. None of these things are possible if left only to me. Trust me, I would mess them up. And that's not to say there hasn't been struggles in this calendar year either, because there has. We have dealt with sick babies, feeling distant from the Lord at times, overwhelmed, busy, having to get a section of my scalp cut out because of a precancerous melanoma spot, bouts with depression, financial woes, and I even have shoulder surgery next week. But none of these things—not even one—can deter us from our mission to serve Him faithfully because of the faithfulness that He has shown us.

We are not perfect—far, far from it. But He loves us and uses us anyway. What could ever be better than knowing that, despite your huge mistakes and minor mess-ups in life, He took your shame and nailed it to a tree and still calls you by name? He still wants to hear from you. He still wants to pour out His Spirit onto you and wash His favor over you. He still wants you to have a relationship with Him, and He wants you to tell Him, "Father, I'm available."

Have you expressed to God your willingness to be fully available for His kingdom?

If not, do it. If so, do it again!

What holds you back or scares you from praying this "I'm available" prayer?

When did you last share or display great faith in King Jesus while surrounded by unbelievers?

By yourself, as a family, or with your small group, would you just pray about being available?

8

Sold Out

What do you think of when you hear the term *sold out*? Maybe you're like me and think about a football or baseball game. Maybe you think about a concert, or the newest tech gadget, and when you go to buy it, it's sold out.

The phrase "sold out" can be defined like this: If a shop is "sold out" of something, it has sold all of it that it had. But if *you* are "sold out," that would make you a "sellout," and a sellout can be defined as "A betrayal, especially through a secret agreement." That's me. That's where I am at this point in my life, and I'm putting all the blame on God. I'm sold out; I'm a sellout, and it's all because of Him. And it's all *for* Him. But it's not in secret.

I do have failures, and I do have struggles, but at the core of my being, I'm a straight-up sellout. Look back to the definition: "a betrayal." The world wants you. All of you. Every single day you are bombarded with ways in which you can indulge in more of what the world says is awesome. Everything is all about Numero Uno: you.

Buy this giant house and this giant TV that you can't afford. Have sex with as many people as you want. Get drunk and party on the weekends with no inhibitions. Have an affair, have an abortion, or just have it all. Step on anyone to get ahead. Don't care for people because they are from a different country or ethnicity than you, and, oh yeah—vote for me.

This is partially why I'm a sellout. This is what I'm betraying. I'm selling out what the world calls for my life and buying into what God has called upon it. What should we be betraying that the world says we need or deserve? Just look at a magazine shelf in any grocery store or bookstore, and you can see what we are supposed to have—by the world's standards.

They tell you that you need more sex, easier hookups. They tell you that you need to invest money here. You deserve this luxury car or this place to retire and live the good life. You need to look this way, enjoy this, or love that, and, above all, you need to put yourself first and do whatever it takes to make you happy.

Is this *really* what we are called to, though? Is this how Jesus spent His time on this planet? If He is who we should be looking to for how to live a holy life and who we should strive to be like, are the things of this world that we sometimes hold onto so dearly holding us back from doing that? Aren't we to trust and call on Him and His Spirit to mold us into what He intends His children to be? Listen to the apostle Paul:

> For God has not called us for impurity, but in
> holiness. Therefore whoever disregards this,

disregards not man but God, who gives his
Holy Spirit to you. (1 Thessalonians 4:7–8 ESV)

He has called you to live a holy life and to be a sellout
against the world and all in for His kingdom. I'm sure you
know someone who is this kind of person. They are someone
who loves God and seems radical in their faith but is full of
joy and hope. Maybe you are that person, or maybe you're not,
but you'd like to be. We can just look in Scripture for what it
means to be sold out against the world and for God.

Nehemiah

One of my favorite stories in the Old Testament is that of
Nehemiah. Nehemiah lived as a cupbearer for King Artaxerxes
of the Persian Empire. This prestigious position reveals
something of Nehemiah's upright character. He was also a
Jew and a servant of God.

When Nehemiah heard about the walls of Jerusalem
being torn down, he was heartbroken. He asked King
Artaxerxes for permission to go back to Jerusalem and
rebuild the walls and was granted that wish. Then he set
out on his mission to reestablish the holy city and bring
glory to God.

This was no easy task, though, and it was made even harder
by strong opposition that was coming in during the time of the
rebuilding. This guy, Sandballat, hated Jews and did not want
the walls to be rebuilt or for the Jews to be allowed to worship
and sacrifice there. He got some other haters riled up for his

cause, and they plotted against Nehemiah and his workers. They didn't just want to thwart their plans of rebuilding the wall, but verse eleven of chapter four tells us that they also wanted to kill them in order to stop the work!

Nehemiah, though, was not deterred. He prayed to God and stationed men with swords and bows at different places to keep watch so that the work could continue. The opposition didn't stop, and "Sandy and the gang" sent messengers to Nehemiah four different times, trying to coax him into meeting them so they could do him harm. They wanted to threaten and scare him into quitting his mission to rebuild the walls and serve God.

But Nehemiah would not be scared into submission or moved by fear or timidity. Our family verse that we adopted this year in my home is found in the middle of this story.

> And I sent messengers to them, saying, "I am doing a great work and I cannot come down. Why should the work stop while I leave it and come down to you?" (Nehemiah 6:3 ESV)

Not much further down, just a few verses later, Nehemiah says,

> For they all wanted to frighten us, thinking, 'Their hands will drop from the work, and it will not be done." But now, O God, strengthen my hands. (Nehemiah 6:9 ESV)

This is why I love this story of Nehemiah. Nothing could bring him down off that wall. He was not rattled by the world. No matter what was going on around him, what kind of opposition he faced, or slander that was sent his way, he would not stop his mission to bring glory to God.

Life on Mission

You and I have a work and a mission to bring glory to God too. And this world is full of people trying to get you to stop, trying to throw slander your way and get you to come down off that wall so you do not finish the work that God has set out for you.

If you aren't sure that God has a plan for you, believe me, He does. You just have to trust Him and follow Jesus wherever He leads. Don't worry about the ridicule that may come your way or the fear of being hated. Don't be stuck in fear, and don't stop serving God because of these temporary feelings.

Francis Chan, in his book *You and Me Forever*,[5] talks about this with great understanding:

> Sometimes people are paralyzed by fear of failure. They are so afraid that they might do the wrong thing that they do nothing. We need to learn to err on the side of action, because we tend to default to negligence. So many won't do anything unless they hear a voice from heaven telling them precisely what to do. Why not default to action until you hear a voice

from heaven telling you to wait? ... we rarely
recognize the sin of omission.

Why not err on the side of action? Why not be sold out for
the cause of Christ and give up anything in this world to live
the life He intended for you? Why be scared of what could
happen? If you trust in Him and believe in His promises of an
eternal life with Him as the reward, who shall you fear? Do you
truly believe that? If you do, what's seriously holding you back?

Nehemiah believed in the promises of God, and he prayed
them in his book, twice. He didn't let anything stop him in
his mission, and neither should you. He didn't let anything
or anyone get in the way of taking action, and neither should
you. We must not be afraid and live scared of what this world
may think because you are called by a King, and His kingdom
is not of this world.

There will be times when you are made fun of, called
ridiculous, are scolded, or, even worse, threatened, possibly
killed. That is what standing up for your faith has come to in
many parts of the world today. But it can't stop you from your
mission for the Most High God. It didn't stop Jesus from His
mission for you.

Jesus was called names, threatened, plotted against, and
killed. But He would not be pushed off His mission to glorify
God the Father and save you from sin and death—not even
when He was nailed onto the cross and lifted up for all to see,
yelled at and scolded. He could have called a legion of angels
and wiped the place clean, but His mission was set out before
Him and He would not be moved. No matter what.

This is what we're called to: to bring glory to the Father and the Lord Jesus Christ. You are called to be sold out for Him, to live a holy life.

> Therefore, preparing your minds for action, and being sober-minded, set your hope fully on the grace that will be brought to you at the revelation of Jesus Christ. As obedient children, do not be conformed to the passions of your former ignorance, but as he who called you is holy, you also be holy in all your conduct, since it is written, "You shall be holy, for I am holy." (1 Peter 1:13–16 ESV)

How does this short passage strike you? We're called to be holy. It talks of the perfect grace that we will receive at the coming of the Lord Jesus and that we are His children. Is this not mind-bending news? How amazing! To add to that, Scripture says we will be raised in His glory (Colossians 3:1–4). Shouldn't who you will be truly affect who you are now?

By His grace, you have been called to this. Pray to Him, listen for Him, seek Him, and run toward the things that He has planned for you. Don't be sluggish; don't just sit back and wait. Don't be afraid of anything because He is in control. His plans will prevail, and His will always comes to pass. He knows all. He uses all things to bring about His glorious story. If you ever start to doubt or walk in fear, be reminded of His great power.

Do you not know? Do you not hear? Has it not been told you from the beginning? Have you not understood from the foundations of the earth? It is he who sits above the circle of the earth, and its inhabitants are like grasshoppers; who stretches out the heavens like a curtain, and spreads them like a tent to dwell in; who brings princes to nothing, and makes the rulers of the earth as emptiness.

Scarcely are they planted, scarcely sown, scarcely has their stem taken root in the earth, when he blows on them, and they wither, and the tempest carries them off like stubble. To whom then will you compare me, that I should be like him? says the Holy One. Lift up your eyes on high and see: who created these? He who brings out their host by number, calling them by name, by the greatness of his might, and because he is strong in power not one is missing. (Isaiah 40:21–26 ESV)

He is the One who has called you. He raises up authorities and crumbles them with just a breath. He calls the stars by name. And He holds you in His righteous hand, with a plan for your life. He has the power to save you and send you out into the world with good works that bring Him glory.

What does this look like for you? It could mean serving the homeless or refugee community in your city. It could mean selling many of your possessions in order to give more to the church or to missionaries. It could mean serving at your local church in ways you never have. It also could mean letting go of things that you don't want to part with.

He may call you into letting go of anxieties about Muslim people and for you to share a relationship and the Gospel with them. He may call you into reaching out to the LGBT community and showing them the love of Christ, when you know that you hold hate and slander in your heart against them. He may call you to leave the comforts of this extremely blessed and rich society and go live in a third world country, sharing His name with people who have never heard it. He may call you out of your comfort zone, away from your Netflix, away from your Facebook and other social media accounts, away from your smartphone, your abundance of family time, and comfort at your workplace into living for things eternal.

He might call you to those things, but there are things you can be promised that He will call you to. Jesus does say that anyone who wants to follow Him must pick up their cross and follow Him. Carrying a cross to your death is no easy walk. Jesus does call you to the Great Commission (Matthew 28:19–20), to make disciples. Jesus does call you to never deny His name before others. And Jesus does call you to believe in Him.

> Truly, truly, I say to you, whoever hears my word and believes in him who sent me has eternal life. He does not come into judgement, but has passed from death to life. (John 5:24 ESV)

93

Believe in Jesus and have eternal life (John 3:16). Eternal life—that is a pretty big concept. But as a concept that because of the love that my wife and I hold for our King, we are devoted to live by it. We will give up our lives because He gave up His for us. How could we do any less?

A king deserves honor, and the King of kings deserves supreme honor. He deserves your best for Him. If even an earthly king asked you to do something, chances are you would do your best to comply. How much more should that ring true for the King who has granted you eternal life with Him in glory forever? That's my King. I wonder: Do you know Him? (There's a plug for Dr. S.M. Lockridge for you.)

Jesus paid our ransom so we could be with Him and in His love now and for eternity. And He paid your ransom for the same thing. You are made in His image, and He knows you by name. He loves you. He wants your confidence to be found in Him.

Will you be sold out for God's kingdom? Will you be joyful and obedient with the call that He has placed on you as Nehemiah was? I desperately want you to feel that perfect love and to live in the joy that comes from knowing Him and following Him, no matter the consequence. I want you to spend all of your days left on this earth living in the fullness of life that comes from Him and holding to the promises that He has given to you to enjoy Him for eternity.

I want you to be with Jesus forever. Forever. That is quite a thought because *forever* is a very long time.

We've been walking in the perspective of carrying this Jesus-authored stone for a few chapters now. Explain the differences in your two stones. What do you love most about who that makes you?

Is there a great work that God is calling you to as He did with Nehemiah?

What is it?

Are you sold out for God to accomplish this task?

Have you spent enough time with God to know His calling for you?

What does it really mean to you to honor the King *now* and *forever*?

9

The Grand Story

Forever.

Eternity.

Do you ever think about these things? Have you ever tried to wrap your mind around those concepts? If you're like me and have, it will boggle your mind and almost make you dizzy.

I think a good correlation to the reality of eternity is the vastness of space. Trying to understand and wrap your head around how big the universe is can make you a similar kind of dizzy and baffled, as can thinking about *forever*.

The universe is huge. Like really, really huge. Think about the Voyager 1 spacecraft that NASA sent out back in 1977. It took more than thirty-five years, traveling at more than thirty-six thousand mph for it to leave our solar system. Just our solar system! So far, Voyager has traveled more than twelve billion miles. That's just to get out of our galactic neighborhood. That's not even getting close to the next closest star because that would take a mind-boggling amount of time. The closest star is more than 4.2 light years away, and a light year is more than 5.88 trillion miles. I'm not qualified to do that kind of math.

None of these figures and distances holds a candle to eternity. It is, though, the closest thing I can think of when contemplating such things. That is how big our God is. He is the one who spoke this universe into being, and He is the one who knows how many breaths you have left. But your story or mine isn't all there is. This life, or even the history of this world, is not the grand story. Eternity is the grand story of God. His eternal kingdom is the focal point, with His glory reigning triumphantly. It will never finish being written. And you get to be a part of it.

The stone I can't put down is my history. It's done—it's written in stone. Nothing I can do will change the things of my past. But my life now and subsequently my eternity are the stone that I won't put down. I cling to the promises given to me in the Word of God and the eternal life that I get to have with Him.

He is the One who fearfully and wonderfully made me. He is the One who knows the number of my days, and He is the One who I wish to be with when I step out of this life and into forever. Like I said, forever is a long time. And where would I rather be in the vastness of forever than in the welcoming, warm, and loving arms of my Savior?

Jesus loves you way more than you can even begin to dream. That love is connected to the perfect love that He, the Father, and the Holy Spirit share, have shared from eternity past, and will share into the eternal future. All for One and One for all. The Triune God.

This huge dynamic of love and how it manifests in Jesus for us to see is no more evident, I think, than in the following verse in the book of Hebrews:

> Looking to Jesus, the founder and perfecter of
> our faith, who for the joy that was set before
> him endured the cross, despising the shame,
> and is seated at the right hand of the throne of
> God. (Hebrews 12:2 ESV)

You can view the love that Jesus has in this verse in a couple of different contexts. "For the joy set before Him endured the cross ..." You are part of that joy. He knew you before the formation of the world. All things are created through Him and for Him (Colossians 1), and that includes you. His love for you, to save you for an eternity away from Him, gave Him joy. He knew He would endure that immense pain and suffering of the cross as well as the agony of separation from the perfect shared love with the Father, all for you, me, and all who put their faith and trust in Him and follow Him.

That is love. That is a kind of deeply rooted love that is hard to wrap your head around. But there is another kind of love in that verse too—the love that is perfectly shared between the Son and the Father. Jesus knows the grand story of eternity. He knew the grand story for the world before He set it into motion, and He knows the grand story that is coming.

Jesus and the Father share a perfect love. The Father has given Jesus all authority and does so lovingly. Jesus submits to the will of the Father and does so lovingly. Jesus also knows that, in the end, we will all be together, singing praises, sitting at a dinner table with Him (Revelation 19:9), and worshipping, saying, "Salvation belongs to our God who sits on the throne, and to the Lamb!" (Revelation 7:10 ESV).

Jesus knew that His death on the cross would ultimately bring worship to the throne of God by the rebels of creation. The people who would put their love and trust in His life, death, burial, and resurrection would get to be in eternity, lifting up songs of praise.

This was the joy that was set before Him to endure the cross—this eternal perspective, this grand story outline that He knows, and this love that He shares with the Father. What a beautiful picture. His love for you is enduring, and His perfect love for God's glory is all wrapped in one statement in His eternal Word.

Do you believe this to be true? Do you believe that the love God has for Himself is the same love that He has for you (John 17:23)? If you don't, I pray that you search what you really believe, deep down, and ask questions. Really think about what this life means and what the purpose of it all is. I pray that you search for truth and meaning and love. And I trust that your search will lead you to the Savior of your soul.

Answer His Invitation

This isn't a closed-off group. This is the house of God, where arms are open wide, accepting you no matter your past, no matter what is written on your stone that you can't put down. If you are searching for truth and love in Christ, ready to repent of your sins, give your life over to the Life Giver, and be a part of His body, His bride, that He will walk with in eternity, then you are welcome in this house. Jesus says,

> Behold, I stand at the door and knock. If anyone hears my voice and opens the door, I will come in to him and eat with him, and him with me. The one who conquers, I will grant him to sit with me on my throne, as I also conquered and sat down with my Father on his throne. (Revelation 3:20–21 ESV)

He is at the door. He is knocking. Will you open it to Him and dine with Him? He is willing to give you a seat at the throne. The work for that to happen has already been done. The ball is in your court.

Many times in the Christian culture people see Jesus at their door; they see Him standing there and knocking. They are in church, know the Christian lingo, and do some volunteering, but it's like they have the main door open and the screen door closed. They can see His glory shining into the house through the screen door, and that is enough for them. But opening the door and allowing Him to come in is just too much to ask for. Don't leave Him behind the screen door. He deserves to be King over your life, and I want you at the banquet table at the end of time.

If you are a part of His body, this church, is this evident in your life? Like we talked about in the last chapter, are you totally sold out for God's glory and God's kingdom? Are you willing to give up everything in order to follow Him?

What's in Front?

That is what Jesus asked of the young rich man in Matthew 19:16–22. The young man asked Jesus how he could have eternal life. Jesus told him to keep the commandments, and the young man explained that he does that—he obeys the rules. But this young man knew something was still missing. He knew he was still lacking whatever it was to have eternal life. He asks, and Jesus tells him, "Go, sell what you possess and give to the poor, and you will have treasure in heaven; and come, follow me" (Matthew 19:21 ESV).

The man was placing something before Jesus and eternal life with Him. Jesus knew what it was and called him out on it. You might not be placing money in front of Jesus, although a lot of us do in the Western culture, maybe without even fully realizing it, but there is a chance you are placing something else in front of Him.

You could be placing pride in front of Him. Maybe you're keeping the "rules" well, like this young man, and that has grown into something that you now put in front of Jesus. You think you have now earned your way into His presence instead of His grace being the only way.

You could be placing relationships in front of Jesus. He may be calling you into a ministry or maybe even the mission field, but you are refusing to go because you have a new girlfriend or boyfriend, or maybe you just don't want to give up your comfortable TV time with your family on Thursday nights.

You could be placing your job, your illness, your material things, or even yourself before Jesus. And He is telling you that those things will never give you freedom, they will never give you a newness of life here and now, and they will never get you eternal life with Him.

There will be sacrifices in following Him. There was for all of the apostles, there was for Stephen in the book of Acts, and there still is today. But these sacrifices are worth it to be with Him forever and to play the part laid out for you in His grand story.

Victory

All it takes for you to inherit salvation and eternal life is to believe in Him, trust that He knows best, and follow Him with joyful obedience. You don't have to win battles on your own because Jesus has already fought those and won them for you. Even though you have a stone that you can't put down, that you carved out of sin and shame, He died for you. Paul expounds on this in Ephesians when he writes,

> But God, being rich in mercy, because of the great love with which he loved us, even when we were dead in our trespasses, made us alive together with Christ—by grace you have been saved—and raised up with him and seated us with him in the heavenly places in Christ Jesus,

> so that in the coming ages he might show the
> immeasurable riches of his grace in kindness
> toward us in Christ Jesus. For by grace you have
> been saved through faith. And it is not your own
> doing; it is a gift of God ... (Ephesians 2:4–8 ESV)

He is so rich in His mercy for you that, while you still stand here holding that stone you can't put down, the one you authored, He died for you to make you alive again and gives you a new life, a new stone, that He is authoring for you into His grand story. Not only that, but this is a done deal. You are sealed in His promise; the battle has been won. Look at the past-tense verbiage: "And *raised* up with him and *seated* us ..." (emphasis added). This shows you that within His eternal and all-knowing view of the grand story, if you are found in Him, you have already won.

Sin, fear, and shame are not found in you because you have already been raised up and seated with Jesus. You live this life and go through trials and endure sacrifices and hard times *because* of this victory, not *for* it. The Victor already reigns.

He has the grand story planned, and it is in motion as you read this book. I pray that you are living to be a part of that story—an eternal party, with Jesus as the host! What more could you want?

Your invitation to this party has not expired. It stays open until your eyes close for the last time. Think about where you want them to open for the first time in eternity.

Don't be caught up in your story. Know that there is more for you. There is more for me. I know that the story of Joe is no story at all. But the story of Christ is an amazing one that I get to be in. I'd rather be a background actor for the grand story than the star in the story of me.

God is all-knowing. He is all-powerful. He is love. He is eternal. He is the Author of salvation and the Author of the grand story. He is standing at the door and knocking, with your invitation into the grand story in hand, with your specific role written right on it.

Open the door and take it.

How does it make you feel to see Christ's love for you *and* for the glory of the Father in His joyful enduring of the cross?

Are you possibly placing anything in front of Jesus? If so, what?

Are you eager for your seat at the banquet with your King?

How does this play into how you're living your life right now?

How have your two stones turned out? How do they look? Different? Similar? The same?

How can the story of the stones you can't put down speak to someone else's life?

Conclusion

I pray that this book has been a blessing to you and has done nothing other than bring glory to God in showing His work in this sinner's life and allowing you chances to look inward into your own life and to walk with Jesus the Lord. I was intentional in how I wrote, what I wrote about, and how much I put in. There is a reason why there are only four chapters about my stone that I *can't* put down, which in this book covers a ten-year span of time, and that there are five chapters about my stone that I *won't* put down, which cover a five-year span of my life and then, obviously, my future with God.

He can do so much more with your life than you ever could dream of doing on your own. Jesus gives purpose and life to you when you disregard what this world wants from you and you put on His truth and love. The stone that you hold in your hand with your past written on it does not have to be who you are forever. The stone of my past is certainly not who I am now. But it is my story—and my story and your story can show the glory of God. Don't let the invitation stay outside the door. Be thankful that telling your story can mean that you tell of Jesus. I pray that your story is inseparable from Him. Without Him, there is hardly any full story at all.

Even if you're going through some things right now, know that He is with you. Like we talked about in the last chapter, He is working all things into His grand story, including you. It may seem hard right now, but take comfort in the promises of Scripture that hold true.

> Do not lose heart. Though our outer self is wasting away, our inner self is being renewed day by day. For this light momentary affliction is preparing for us an eternal weight of glory beyond all comparison ... (2 Corinthians 4:16–17 ESV)

Hold true to that. He is working for you an eternal weight of glory beyond anything you could ever imagine. He breathes out galaxies, and He knows all of man's thoughts effortlessly. He can promise you glory in eternity. He will come through on that promise.

Love Him and let Him write your new story on the stone that you won't put down. Focus on Him all of your days, and follow His lead. You wrote your past in stone. Now let Him write your future in it. Will you please reflect over this book and think? Think about what your story is, what your stones are. When was the turning point? When did you start carrying the stone that you won't put down? If you haven't started, now is the time.

I'm reminded of a verse that I have been coming back to a lot lately. It has reshaped parts of my life and brought me into closer relationship with Him. I have it taped to my car dashboard, and I'd like to share it with you as we close this book together. It comes from the book of Psalms.

> One thing have I asked of the LORD, that will I seek after: that I may dwell in the house of the LORD all the days of my life, to gaze upon the beauty of the LORD and to inquire in his temple. (Psalm 27:4 ESV)

This verse has moved me into worship, and as we close, I hope it does you too. We have already talked about how much God loves you and knows you (Psalm 139), and I want you to seek after Him and know Him. Let Him be the Scribe for the stone you can't put down. What better way to do that than to seek after Him? Let there be just one thing that you ask of Him—to seek Him, dwell in His house all your life, gaze upon His beauty, and know His will.

The beauty of Jesus is unmatched. There is no competition. Please know this to be true. Don't be ashamed of the stone you can't put down, and don't be ashamed of the stone you won't put down. It can all glorify our King. Will you use what is left of your life to do just that? Hold the stones that you can't put down and glorify your King.

You are the reason for the stone you *can't* put down. *He* is the reason for the stone you *won't* put down. Praise God.

Acknowledgments

I am in debt to such a great number of people for this book even becoming a reality. I do not know how to name everyone I would like to, so if I forget you, please don't be offended.

I thank God for my wife. You are beautiful on the inside and out, and I am privileged to run this race with you. Thank you for putting up with my crazy ideas, incessant reading, and childish humor. You are irreplaceable. You are loved.

I thank God for my three sons. You boys are the twinkle of your daddy's eye and a true source of my joy. Life is so much more fun with you all in it.

I thank God for my extended families—the Stewarts, Pomerleaus, and Carters. I love you all deeply and value your relationships.

I thank God for my local church body of Liberty Christian Fellowship. I am grateful that it is a place where nothing is put higher than the worship of God in Jesus Christ. I am thankful for being trusted with a leadership position within this great body and for the relationships that are grown inside and outside of those walls.

I thank God for everyone who preordered this book on Kickstarter to help get this project off the ground. I am incredibly indebted to you for purchasing a book you had little clue about. Thank you for believing in me.

I thank God for WestBow Press. Thank you for being so helpful in this process and for your dedication to publishing manuscripts that glorify God.

I thank God for Frank Kresen. Thank you for your diligence and patience in editing my first manuscript. This book would not be the same without your expertise.

I thank God for Amanda Lee. Thank you for putting your extraordinary talents on display to make this book look appealing from a shelf. You are a blessing to our family!

Thank you to Kearney Landscape Materials. Your generosity in donating to this project has not gone unnoticed or unappreciated. Thank you for the stones!

I thank God for the countless men and women around the world who have invested time into my life and helped lead me to a better understanding of Scripture and who God is. I am thankful for every relationship that honors God and enriches my life as iron sharpening iron. I am so blessed.

I thank God for Midwestern Baptist Theological Seminary. I am humbled to be a part of such a God-honoring group of people who exist *For The Church.*

Most of all, I thank God for cleansing me of all my shame and guilt. I thank Him for washing away every sin I have ever committed, or will ever commit. The grace and love of Jesus is unrivaled, and in the depths of who I am, my prayer is that, in knowing Him, my life may bring glory and honor to His name. You, Lord, deserve all praise from every nation and every tongue, for You are the purpose of our worship.

Notes

[1] "A Shrub and a Grub," Tim Fritson sermon, Liberty Christian Fellowship, Liberty, Missouri, October 18, 2015. accessed March 12, 2016, http://lcfliberty.org/media--resources/teaching/messages/media-item/129/a-shrub-and-a-grub.

[2] Timothy Keller, *The Prodigal God: Recovering the Heart of the Christian Faith* (New York: Riverhead, 2011) Print.

[3] Louie Giglio, *The Comeback: It's Not Too Late And You're Never Too Far* (Nashville: Thomas Nelson, 2015) 71.

[4] "Comfort Must Fall." Louie Giglio sermon, Passion City Church, Atlanta, GA, August 3, 2014. accessed March 12, 2016. http://passioncitychurch.libsyn.com/comfort-must-fall

[5] Francis Chan and Lisa Chan, *You And Me Forever: Marriage In Light Of Eternity* (San Francisco: Claire Love Publishing, 2014) 16.